John Wesley Freese

Historic Houses and Spots in Cambridge, Massachusetts, and

near-by Towns

John Wesley Freese

Historic Houses and Spots in Cambridge, Massachusetts, and near-by Towns

ISBN/EAN: 9783337152215

Printed in Europe, USA, Canada, Australia, Japan

Cover: Foto ©ninafisch / pixelio.de

More available books at **www.hansebooks.com**

Historic Houses

and Spots

IN

Cambridge, Massachusetts

AND

Near-by Towns

BY

J. W. FREESE

PRINCIPAL OF THE WASHINGTON SCHOOL, CAMBRIDGE

"God sifted a whole nation that He might send choice grain over into this wilderness."

BOSTON, U.S.A., AND LONDON
GINN & COMPANY, PUBLISHERS
The Athenæum Press
1898

PREFACE.

For more than twelve years I have been searching out and studying the most ancient homes of Cambridge and other historic towns and cities near by, for the benefit of the pupils under my charge. As we made our annual rounds, the disappearance of old "landmarks" became, year by year, more noticeable, and thus it occurred to me that a favor might be conferred upon many by giving in this modest little work definite location and brief account of the most famous old houses. To the schoolchildren of Cambridge and other places this work may be specially useful, supplemented as it is by original and picturesque views, and also by brief references to famous persons with whose names some of the houses are associated.

It has been my conviction for years that the study of local history is the best introduction to the study of more general history, and in this view I have been confirmed by the ever-increasing historical pilgrimages, and above all by the testimony of great men who have made the study of history their profession. Prof. H. B. Adams, of Johns Hopkins University, says:

"History, like charity, begins at home. . . . The best students of universal history are those who know some one country or some one subject well. The family, the hamlet, the neighborhood, the community, the parish, the village, town, city, county, and State are historically the ways by which men have approached national and international life."

The facts I present have not been evolved from "inner consciousness," for, although I have had access to original sources, I have also gleaned freely from Drake's *Landmarks* and various local histories. My indebtedness is, therefore, easily seen and heartily acknowledged.

So far as both cover the same ground, *Historic Houses* and Walker's *Historical Map* may be advantageously used together.

JOHN W. FREESE.

CAMBRIDGE, MASS., 1897.

NOTE. — It is probably true that the writer has overlooked some historic house or spot that, in the mind of the local antiquarian, may be considered important. If so, correspondence with respect to it or to any error that may have been made is earnestly solicited, to the end that this book may be made as useful as possible, in case a second edition should be called for.

J. W. F.

CONTENTS.

	PAGE
INTRODUCTION	1, 2
ARLINGTON	35–41
BEDFORD	59–62
BEVERLY	127, 128
BILLERICA	63–65
BOSTON	82–94
CAMBRIDGE	3–34
CHARLESTOWN	139, 140
CHELSEA	118–121
CONCORD	52–58
DANVERS	129–131
DEDHAM	106, 107
DORCHESTER	95–97
HINGHAM	109, 110
IPSWICH	134
JAMAICA PLAIN	104, 105
LANCASTER	66
LEXINGTON	42–51
LYNN	136, 137
MALDEN	71
MEDFORD	67–69
MILTON	98–100

CONTENTS.

	PAGE
MISCELLANEOUS OLD HOUSES	141–144
QUINCY . .	108
ROXBURY	101–103
SALEM .	122–126
SAUGUS .	. 135
SOMERVILLE	. 75–81
STONEHAM	. 74
SUDBURY .	111–114
SWAMPSCOTT	. 138
TOPSFIELD	132, 133
WATERTOWN	115–117
WINCHESTER	70
WOBURN	72, 73

LIST OF ILLUSTRATIONS.

	PAGE
THE ADAMS HOUSES	108
THE AUSTIN HOUSE	3
THE GOVERNOR BELLINGHAM MANSION	118
"THE BISHOP'S PALACE"	15
THE OLD BOWLDER	44
THE BRATTLE HOUSE	5
THE BROWN HOUSE	115
THE PARSON CAPEN HOUSE	132
CHRIST CHURCH (Cambridge)	13
CHRIST CHURCH (Boston)	93
THE CRADOCK HOUSE	68
THE HOME OF EMERSON	56
THE EVERETT HOUSE	96
THE OLD FAIRBANKS HOUSE	106
THE OLD FIRST CHURCH	124
FANEUIL HALL	88
THE HILL-BOARDMAN HOUSE	135
THE LEE HOUSE	4
THE ABEL LOCKE HOUSE	37
THE LOWELL HOUSE	12
THE LONGFELLOW HOUSE	7
THE OLD MANSE	57

LIST OF ILLUSTRATIONS.

	PAGE
MASSACHUSETTS HALL	21
THE MINUTE-MAN	54
THE MUNROE TAVERN	47
THE REBECCA NOURSE HOUSE	129
THE OLD STATE HOUSE	86
THE OLD SOUTH CHURCH	84
THE PIERCE HOUSE	95
THE OLD POWDER HOUSE	79
THE PRATT HOUSE	120
THE PRESIDENT'S HOUSE	17
THE ISAAC ROYALL HOUSE	67
THE RUGGLES HOUSE	11
THE SALTONSTALL-WHIPPLE HOUSE	134
"SUNDAY SCHOOL" HOUSE	128
BENJAMIN THOMPSON HOUSE	72
THE SAMUEL TUFTS HOUSE	76
THE VASSALL MONUMENT	9
THE VOSE HOUSE	98
WARD HOUSE	123
THE WASHINGTON ELM	18
THE WATERHOUSE HOUSE	20
THE WAYSIDE INN	111
A WOLF PIT	136
THE AMOS WYMAN HOUSE	64

HISTORIC HOUSES AND SPOTS

IN

CAMBRIDGE, MASSACHUSETTS, AND NEAR-BY TOWNS.

THE citizens of Cambridge, now over 80,000 in number, might well lay claim to several unique distinctions for the city of which they are so justly proud. First, it must be remembered that Cambridge is the seat of the oldest and most distinguished university in America.

The opportunity thus offered for broad learning and generous culture is the probable reason for a second distinction : viz., that Cambridge has lately become also the seat of Radcliffe College. Here are also two divinity schools besides the one directly connected with the University. The spirit of emulation fostered by these institutions of learning, together with the influence of several excellent preparatory schools, has undoubtedly had a most beneficial effect upon the public schools and should receive a measure of credit for their efficiency. The public schools of Cambridge are noted for their excellence. As Cambridge was contemporaneous with Boston in her settlement, and was also for a time the seat of government, she has left the impress of her hand upon the fundamental law of our beloved Commonwealth.

Her soil was also the first rallying-point of patriots to repel British aggression, and here Washington first unsheathed his sword in defence of our liberties.

In fact it is a matter of some surprise that, as Lexington and Concord have contended with some spirit as to which was entitled to the larger share of honor for the glorious deeds of April 19, 1775, Cambridge should not also have put in her claim. She could have done so with a good show of reason, for the first detachment of British troops for Concord, as well as their reënforcements, passed through Cambridge. Those of the early morning were pursued the whole distance to Concord by a company of Cambridge men, about seventy in number, who "fully participated in the perils and the glory of that day." A company of fifty minute-men, twenty-five of whom were Cambridge men, had previously been formed and were also actively engaged on that day. "The conflict has generally been called the 'Concord Fight' or the 'Lexington Battle'; but the carnage was greater in this town than in any other, — greater, indeed, than in all others combined, if it be true, as has been stated by a diligent investigator, that 'at least twenty-two of the Americans, and probably more than twice that number of the British, fell in West Cambridge.' Four native citizens were killed near the Jacob Watson House (now standing) in North Cambridge. Thus we have twenty-six, or more than half of all the Americans whose lives were sacrificed on that memorable day."

Cambridge bore her part well not only on April 19, but during the siege of Boston. With a fort at Lechmere's Point, another — Fort Washington — on Waverly Street (restored and enclosed by the city with a costly iron fence), and another at Captain Patrick's island, the town may be said to have been a fortified camp.

Her eminent citizens, native and adopted, are indeed a crowning distinction. They need not be mentioned. Everybody knows them.

Lastly, Cambridge is the mother of towns, and is proud of her children. At one time her territory comprised Brighton, Newton, Arlington, Lexington, and Billerica.

THE AUSTIN HOUSE.

This interesting old house is now numbered 21 Linnaean Street and was built, in 1657, by Deacon Jonathan Cooper and continued to belong to his descendants for three generations. In the will of Walter, of the third generation, we find these quaint specifications: "I will that my beloved wife, Martha, should have out of my movable property, 40 pounds, lawful money, also my silver cup and my Mare and chair and the best cow and one of the pigs. . . . I also will that she should have the west half of my dwelling house and the liberty of the ovens in t'other room."

It became successively the property of Jonathan Hill, Deacon Frost, and, in 1807, of the late Mrs. Austin, whose husband, Rev. Mr. Seiders, took her name. She died, in 1885, childless.

Cambridge.

THE LEE HOUSE.

This, with one possible exception (the Austin House), is the oldest house now standing in Cambridge.

At the beginning of the war with England it was owned and occupied by Judge Joseph Lee, a rather lukewarm royalist, who lived in Boston during the siege but was allowed to return to his home after the war, where he died in 1802. Of all the historic houses of Cambridge, this, to my mind, if judged by its venerable outward appearance, has the strongest claim to the title of "antique."

It is on Brattle Street, near Appleton Street, and was probably built before 1660.

Cambridge.

THE BRATTLE HOUSE.

This is on Brattle Street (formerly called Tory Row), near Brattle Square. It seems first to have been occupied by a William Brattle, who "was successively physician, preacher, and lawyer." During the siege of Boston it was the headquarters of General Mifflin, who on one occasion entertained here the accomplished Abigail Adams, wife of John Adams, presenting to her his eccentric friend General Charles Lee, together with his (Lee's) dog "Spada."

After the war the property was restored to William Brattle's son, Thomas Brattle, who expended much time and money in cultivating choice flowers and fruits on the grounds that extended from Brattle Square to Ash Street and to the river. For a time Margaret Fuller lived here.

THE GOVERNOR BELCHER HOUSE.

This house is on Brattle Street, corner of Hawthorn. It was built about 1700, and came into the possession of Jonathan Belcher in 1717. He afterwards became Sir Jonathan, and was governor of Massachusetts and New Hampshire from 1730 till 1741.

In 1736 it became the property of Colonel John Vassall, who sold it to his brother, Major Henry, whose widow, Penelope, sister of Isaac Royall, lived in it at the beginning of hostilities. Here Dr. Benjamin Church, the first discovered American traitor who was condemned to exile, was for a time a prisoner. The vessel on which he sailed for the West Indies was not heard from afterward.

This house was probably used as a hospital early in the war of the Revolution. The owner of the house, Mrs. James, states that on one of the old doors may still be seen the name B. Church, Jr., heavily cut in the wood.

THE LONGFELLOW HOUSE.

This Colonial mansion was commonly known as the Craigie House, but is now usually pointed out as the Longfellow House. It is numbered 105 Brattle Street, and was built, about 1759, by Colonel John Vassall the younger. He, being a tory, fled at the beginning of the Revolution. Soon after his flight the house was occupied by Colonel John Glover with his regiment. Washington took possession July 15, 1775, and left it in April, 1776.

Then in succession came Nathaniel Tracy, Thomas Russell, Andrew Craigie (who entertained here the Duke of Kent, father of Queen Victoria), Jared Sparks, Edward Everett, and Joseph E. Worcester of dictionary fame.

Longfellow first roomed here in 1837 and afterward in 1843. After Mrs. Craigie's death he came into full possession of the house. Here nearly all his works were written.

Longfellow's feeling for the old Colonial house was one of the deepest interest and veneration. Miss Longfellow says, "He was never willing to make the slightest change in even the smallest particular, even for comfort or convenience." It stands to-day as it was originally built by Colonel Vassall, with the enlargements by Dr. Craigie. The poet sings:

>   Once, ah! once, within these walls,
>   One whom memory oft recalls,
>   The Father of his Country dwelt.
>   And yonder meadows broad and damp
>   The fires of the besieging camp
>   Encircled with a burning belt.
>   Up and down these echoing stairs,
>   Heavy with the weight of cares,
>   Sounded his majestic tread;
>   Yes, within this very room
>   Sat he in those hours of gloom,
>   Weary both in heart and head.
>   LONGFELLOW.

The room occupied by Washington was a large second-story front room, facing southeast. The room underneath it was used by Washington for his study and later by Longfellow for the same purpose.

Once, during the siege of Boston, Washington entertained Franklin here, concerning whom, on this occasion, General Greene said:

>   "Attention watched his lips,
>   And conviction closed his periods."

THE VASSALL MONUMENT.

This is in the ancient burying-ground, Massachusetts Avenue, near Harvard Square. Its horizontal (red sandstone) slab has cut upon its upper surface a vase and an image of the sun,—a hint of the origin of the name Vassall (vassol).

If rumor can be credited, two slaves were buried here, one at the head, the other at the foot, of the tomb of Madame Vassall.

> In the village churchyard she lies,
> Dust is in her beautiful eyes;
> No more she breathes, nor feels, nor stirs;
> At her feet and at her head
> Lies a slave to attend the dead,
> But their dust is as white as hers.
> LONGFELLOW.

THE LECHMERE OR SEWALL-RIEDESEL HOUSE.

This house formerly stood on Brattle Street, corner of Sparks, but is now the third from the corner, and has been remodeled in recent years.

It was first occupied by Richard Lechmere, former owner of Lechmere's Point, East Cambridge, and afterwards by Jonathan Sewall, both royalists. The spot where it formerly stood should be visited for the sake of the beautiful linden trees so warmly spoken of by Baroness Riedesel. The house was assigned for her use and the baron's after the surrender at Saratoga, in September, 1777, and is often called the Riedesel House. The lindens must have been good-sized trees even then to have elicited encomiums from the baroness at a time when she had so little cause for enthusiasm, her husband being a prisoner.

THE RUGGLES HOUSE.

It is now 175 Brattle Street, and is said to take its name from its builder, one Mr. Ruggles, the last of the king's foresters in America. It descended to his brother, Captain George Ruggles, but passed into the hands of Thomas Fayerweather before the Revolutionary War.

It then became the property of Mr. William Wells, in the possession of whose grandchildren, the Newells, it now is. Mr. Wells had here a private school for boys, three of whom at least have since earned more than a national reputation. Reference is made to James Russell Lowell, William Wetmore Story, and Thomas Wentworth Higginson.

The Ruggles House has a dignity and charm peculiar to itself and is "beautiful for situation."

CHRIST CHURCH.

"We love the venerable house
Our fathers built to God:
In heaven are kept their grateful vows;
Their dust endears the sod."

Christ Church (on Garden Street, opposite the common) was built 1759-1761, and was opened for public worship October 15, 1761, the Rev. East Apthorp being the first minister.

On New Year's Eve, 1775, General Washington held service here, Colonel William Palfrey reading the service. Connecticut troops were quartered here about the time of the battle of Bunker Hill. The body of an English officer, Lieutenant Richard Brown, killed on Prospect Hill, Somerville, was placed beneath this church, where is also the tomb of the Vassall family.

The lead organ-pipes were melted into bullets by the soldiers, the church being tory property. Two pieces of a communion service — a silver flagon and a covered cup — given to King's Chapel, Boston, are now the property of this church.

> Our ancient church! its lowly tower,
> Beneath the loftier spire,
> Is shadowed when the sunset hour
> Clothes the tall shaft in fire;
> It sinks beyond the distant eye
> Long ere the glittering vane,
> High wheeling in the western sky,
> Has faded o'er the plain.
>
> OLIVER WENDELL HOLMES.

THE LOWELL HOUSE.

This interesting old mansion, which is now commonly known as Elmwood, is on Elmwood Avenue, near Mt. Auburn.

It was probably built about the year 1760, and seems to have been owned by John Stratton, of whose heirs it was purchased by Lieutenant-Governor Oliver. It was at one time the home of Governor Elbridge Gerry, one of the signers of the Declaration of Independence, and vice-president of the United States from 1813 to 1814. After the battle of Bunker Hill it was used as a hospital.

It finally became the property of the Rev. Charles Lowell, father of James Russell Lowell, who was born here February 22, 1819. Lowell's study was on the left of the entrance hall, — a large room with its window overlooking "the long green levels among the trees on the lawn." The room back of this, with shelves lining the walls, was used as the poet's library.

"THE BISHOP'S PALACE."

It is 10 Linden Street, and was built, about 1761, by the Rev. East Apthorp, the first minister of Christ Church, and received its title in derision from his persecuting enemies.

It is one of the finest of the old houses of Cambridge. After Mr. Apthorp it became the property of a Mr. John Borland of Boston, who is said to have built the third story the better to accommodate his domestic slaves. It served both as headquarters and barracks for General Putnam and his Connecticut troops till about the time of the battle of Bunker Hill.

After the surrender at Saratoga it became the residence of Burgoyne.

It is now (1897) the home of Professor William H. Niles of the Massachusetts Institute of Technology. The house, set in a large garden, is grand in proportions and architecture, and, as has been justly said, " is fitted in every respect to bear the name which still clings to it."

THE HOLMES HOUSE.

This was a gambrel-roofed house supposed to have been built about 1700. It stood on Cambridge Street, second house from the corner of Massachusetts Avenue, and was torn down about a dozen years ago. It was conveyed to one Jabez Fox in 1707 and by his heirs to Jonathan Hastings and finally to Rev. Abiel Holmes, father of Oliver Wendell Holmes, who was born here August 29, 1809. It was the headquarters of General Ward and, after the battle of Lexington, of the Committee of Safety and for a short time of Washington. Here Benedict Arnold received his commission as colonel, and on the green in front were assembled the troops to listen to prayer, by President Langdon of the College, invoking divine aid in their behalf, preparatory to the battle of Bunker Hill.

The poem "Old Ironsides" was written here.

THE PRESIDENT'S HOUSE.

This quaint old dwelling on Massachusetts Avenue, Harvard Square, is also known as Wadsworth House, and now contains the office of the bursar of the College. It was the home of the presidents of the University for a hundred and twenty-three years, 1726-1849,— President Wadsworth being the first occupant; the others were Holyoke, Locke, Langdon, Willard, Webber, Kirkland, Quincy, and Everett. It was intended as headquarters for Washington. He was escorted from Watertown the 2d of July, 1775, by a company of horse and a large body of mounted civilians to the President's House. For some reason or other he stayed but two weeks and then transferred his effects to the Vassall House, which he seems to have preferred.

In this house the royal governors were entertained on occasions of anniversary celebrations, as were many other persons of dignity and note. Some of the beautiful elms that now cast their shadows upon the old house are said to have been planted by President Willard.

Cambridge.

THE WASHINGTON ELM.

> UNDER THIS TREE
> WASHINGTON
> FIRST TOOK COMMAND
> OF THE
> AMERICAN ARMY
> JULY 3d, 1775.

A hint as to the great age of this tree is given in the fact that Washington had a platform placed within its branches, from which he was enabled to overlook the army encamped on the common.

It is visited annually by a large number of persons from all parts of this country and from abroad, who gaze upon its massive form with mingled feelings of awe and admiration. It is now tenderly cared for, and though the vicissitudes of time have impressed upon it the indelible marks of decay, it is likely to last for many years to come.

> " A goodly elm of noble girth
> That thrice the human span —
> While on their variegated course
> The constant seasons ran —
> Through gale and hail and fiery bolt
> Has stood erect as man."

THE WATERHOUSE HOUSE.

This well-preserved and interesting old house, built in 1753, is numbered 7 Waterhouse Street. It was for many years the home of Dr. Benjamin Waterhouse, who was born at Newport, R. I., in 1754, studied in London, Edinburgh, and Leyden, and was "professor of the theory and practice of physic in the medical school of Harvard College" for thirty years. He introduced the art of vaccination into the colonies, for which he was much persecuted.

The house contains many historic curios, among which may be mentioned a "six-month" clock, the gift of the stamp officer, Peter Oliver, whose granddaughter, Elizabeth, was the doctor's first wife ; also two portraits, — one of the doctor, by Frothingham, and the other of his mother at the age of ninety, by Washington Allston, at the time a student in Harvard College and an occupant of a room in the house.

The present occupant of the house is Miss Mary H. Ware, daughter of the Rev. William Ware.

Cambridge.

MASSACHUSETTS HALL.

Massachusetts Hall (west side of the college yard, south of the Johnston gateway) is the oldest of the college buildings proper now standing, and was erected in 1720, during the presidency of John Leverett.

Holden Chapel is frequently, but erroneously, given the honor of being the oldest, but it was erected in 1745, Edward Holyoke being president. Massachusetts Hall has been the college home of not a few who afterwards became famous. Among these there is one at least whose memory it is a delight to cherish and revere, — Judge Joseph Story, first Dane Professor of law at Harvard, who was at the same time Associate Justice of the Supreme Court of the United States.

THE HICKS HOUSE.

The Hicks House, which is now standing on Dunster Street, corner of Winthrop, was built by John Hicks, who was killed on the day of the battle of Lexington, and whose name is on the monument in the burying-ground adjoining Christ Church.

The spot where he fell is marked with a tablet on Massachusetts Avenue, near Spruce Street:

```
AT THIS PLACE
APRIL 19, 1775
FOUR CITIZENS WERE KILLED
BY BRITISH SOLDIERS
RETREATING FROM LEXINGTON.
```

THE MARGARET FULLER HOUSE.

The house in which Margaret Fuller was born, May 23, 1810, is still standing on the corner of Cherry and Eaton Streets, Cambridgeport, and is visited annually by many persons. America thus far, probably, has not produced a woman intellectually her superior. She was noted as a teacher, as an editor, and as a writer and literary critic. In 1847 she became the wife of the Marquis d'Ossoli of Italy. The vessel on which she was returning to her native land with her husband and young son was wrecked within sight of it, she being among the number lost. Emerson and Hawthorne were her warm friends, and she visited the latter when he was living in the community at Brook Farm, Roxbury.

The number of the house is 69 Cherry Street.

THE HOME OF WASHINGTON ALLSTON.

The house in which Washington Allston, the celebrated painter, lived, while a resident of Cambridge, is not now standing, but was formerly on Magazine Street, corner of Auburn, his studio being nearly opposite. He was born in South Carolina, November 5, 1779, and showed a love for art at an early age. He entered Harvard in 1796, and went to Europe in 1801. In Rome he studied four years, acquiring the name of "the American Titian." He is also known as America's greatest historical painter, many of his most costly works being now possessed by wealthy Boston families. He was twice married, his second wife being a daughter of Chief Justice Francis Dana of Dana Hill, Cambridge. He died in Cambridge on July 9, 1843.

TABLETS.

Since the next best thing to knowing the history of a place is the knowledge of its location, historic spots of interest, which are now marked by tablets, will be designated.

HERE STOOD
THE FIRST SCHOOLHOUSE
OF CAMBRIDGE
BUILT IN 1648.

The tablet with the above inscription is on the west side of Holyoke Street, opposite the home of the Hasty Pudding Club.

In the stone building here erected a school was kept till 1769, when it was removed to the southerly side of Garden Street, a short distance north of Appian Way, and there continued until about 1838.

This was the school (now the Washington) spoken of by Johnson, in 1643, in his "Wonder Working Providence," as " a faire Grammar Schoole."

> SITE OF THE
> FIRST MEETING HOUSE IN CAMBRIDGE.
> ERECTED A.D. 1632.

These words are on the granite foundation of a building on Mt. Auburn Street, corner of Dunster.

"This meeting-house was a plain and simple structure, probably built of logs, and had a thatched roof. The congregation at first were called together by the beating of a drum. Here preached the gifted Hooker for two years, who was styled 'the light of the western churches,' and the pious Thomas Shepard for thirteen years."

In 1642 the first Harvard College commencement exercises were held in this church.

THE HOUSE OF JOHN WATSON.

On the west side of Massachusetts Avenue, near Spruce Street, a tablet is placed, marking the spot where three citizens of Cambridge were killed, April 19, 1775: *viz.*, John Hicks, William Marcy, and Moses Richardson, the last named being the great-grandfather of Captain James P. Richardson. The company commanded by the latter was probably the first company of soldiers to start for the defence of Washington at the beginning of the Great Rebellion in 1861. The house west of the tablet was a witness of the tragedies, and was the home of John Watson, a farmer.

The tablet inscribed as above is on the easterly side of a building numbered 1732 at Harvard Square.

Stephen Daye was succeeded by his son, Matthew, and he, in 1649, by Samuel Green; "and for forty years all the printing done in America was at Cambridge." "About one hundred works bear the Cambridge imprint prior to the year 1700, the chief of which is the Bible translated into the Indian language, by John Eliot, a copy of which is now in the library at Harvard College."

It is worthy of note that printing is still one of the leading industries of Cambridge.

> THOMAS DUDLEY,
> FOUNDER OF CAMBRIDGE,
> GOVERNOR OF MASSACHUSETTS,
> LIVED HERE IN 1630.

This tablet is on Dunster Street, corner of South.

Thomas Dudley was governor four years, deputy governor for thirteen, and assistant governor for eight years, and was major-general of all the forces in 1644. He died in Roxbury, in 1653, at the age of seventy-six years.

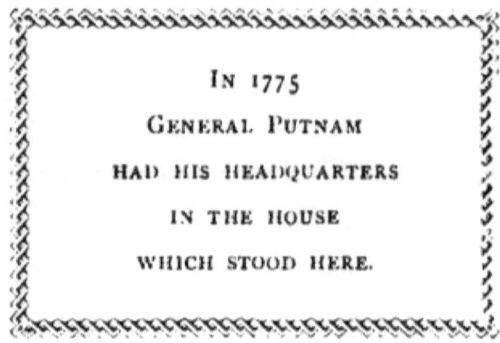

In 1775
General Putnam
had his headquarters
in the house
which stood here.

The house stood on Inman Street, near the City Hall, and was that of Ralph Inman, a Tory, who was arrested in 1776.

It is interesting to note the fact that his daughter became the wife of Captain John Linzee, who was in command of the British man-of-war, "Falcon," stationed in the Charles River at the time of the battle of Bunker Hill, and that their granddaughter became the wife of the historian, Prescott, grandson of Colonel William Prescott, who commanded the Americans at the same battle.

"The crossed swords,"— those of Colonel Prescott and Captain Linzee,— worn during the battle, is an object of interest to be seen at the rooms of the Massachusetts Historical Society, Boston.

> ON THIS SPOT
> IN 1630
> STOOD AN ANCIENT OAK
> UNDER WHICH WERE HELD
> COLONIAL ELECTIONS.
> THIS SCION OF THE
> WASHINGTON ELM
> WAS PLANTED
> MAY, 1896.

The tablet is on the common, the Massachusetts Avenue side, nearly opposite the head of Cambridge Street.

From Colonel T. W. Higginson we learn that there took place under this oak tree a very exciting election contest, in 1637, between the friends of the governor, Sir Henry Vane, whose statue may now be seen in the Boston Public Library, and those of John Winthrop, the latter being victorious largely in consequence of an earnest speech of Rev. John Wilson, first minister of Boston, who stood among the branches of the old oak during the delivery of this speech.

Cambridge.

On the left bank of Charles River, near the Cambridge Hospital, Mount Auburn Street, is a tablet inclosed by an iron fence and bearing the following inscription:

> ON THIS SPOT
> IN THE YEAR 1000
> LEIF ERICKSON
> BUILT HIS HOUSE IN
> VINELAND.

This tablet was placed here by Professor Eben Norton Horsford, whose patient and exhaustive researches led him to believe the territory in this vicinity to be identical with the Vineland of the Northmen.

Farther west are two other spots with rude inclosures, one the supposed site of another Northman's house and the other a paved pathway leading from the river to one of the houses. It is said to be the custom of the people of Iceland and Greenland to-day to construct such pathways.

Professor Horsford was born in Moscow, New York, in 1818, and died January 1, 1893. He was Rumford professor at Harvard from 1847 to 1863. His name is a household word throughout the land in consequence of his useful chemical discoveries and for his broad charities and educational endowments. There came to the knowledge of the author recently an incident in the life of the great professor that deserves to be much emphasized and frequently imitated. On being presented with his tax bill on one occasion, he promptly informed the assessors that it was *too small*, and that he desired to bear his full share of the burden of taxation.

Cambridge.

> PUTNAM SCHOOL.
>
> SITE OF
>
> FORT PUTNAM
>
> ERECTED BY THE AMERICAN FORCES
>
> DEC. 1775
>
> DURING THE SIEGE OF BOSTON.

The site is to be found on the corner of Otis and Fourth Streets, East Cambridge. The fort was a strong one, and was constructed during a bombardment by a British man-of-war only a half-mile distant. A cannon-ball fired from this fort struck the side of the Brattle Street Church, Boston, at some time during the siege, and can now be seen at the rooms of the Massachusetts Historical Society, Boston.

Cambridge.

Our good city is not without articles of historic and literary interest, as may be seen by a visit to the Cambridge Public Library, situated on Broadway, between Irving and Trowbridge Streets.

Among the objects worthy of special mention are:

The manuscript of *The Progress of the World*, by J. R. Lowell; Margaret Fuller's *European Note Book;* manuscript letters of Longfellow, Lowell, Everett, R. H. Dana, and Margaret Fuller — all of Cambridge, — of Washington, Jefferson, and Santa Anna; a silk flag sent to the 38th Massachusetts Regiment by Cambridge ladies; a copy of the *New England Chronicle* of December 14-21, 1775, which was printed in Stoughton Hall, Harvard College. There are also Indian stone implements from Longfellow Park; a Cambridge tax bill of 1790; a cane from the wood of the "Spreading Chestnut Tree," gift of Dr. Lucius R. Paige; shoes worn by the wife of General Washington; and a silk badge worn at Washington's inauguration. These and many more articles of historic value and interest may be seen by teachers and their pupils by making proper previous arrangements with the librarian.

Arlington.

To one familiar with the picturesque topography of Arlington (why could it not have retained its Indian name of Menotomy?) there can be no surprise at the evident contentment of the people with their situation. The "Heights" are visited at almost all seasons of the year for a view almost unsurpassed in its extent and loveliness. Somehow, we cannot hear the name without having visions of pure air and sparkling spring water. Even the robin becomes so enamored of the sheltered nooks and secluded valleys that he is fast forgetting his migratory habits, and actually spends whole winters here.

Best of all, the people are living up to the patriotic traditions of their earlier history, an evidence of which is to be seen in the substantial monuments to the memory of the heroes of the first as well as of the last war.

Arlington has now in good state of preservation a considerable number of houses of the Colonial period.

A modest but interesting one is

THE AMOS WHITTEMORE HOUSE.

It is now numbered 209 Massachusetts Avenue, near the Soldiers' Monument.

Mr. Whittemore was, for the time, a famous inventor, a machine for making wool-cards being his greatest achievement. On this he obtained a patent. Proposals for its renewal came in the time of John Randolph, who said, "Renew it forever, for it is the only machine with a soul." Till recent repairs were made, the old house bore the marks of British bullets.

THE MOLLY CUTTER HOUSE.

For some unknown reason the British manifested particular disfavor toward this house, as they plundered it of a year's supply of candles and built a fire in one of its closets. It is now numbered 333 Massachusetts Avenue, and is next to the Universalist Church.

At 312 Massachusetts Avenue is an old house that claims to have been built prior to 1776. The bakery business seems to have been carried on here from the first.

THE SAMUEL RUSSELL HOUSE.

This quaint house was built by the grandfather of an old lady now living in it at the age of eighty-nine years.

It is numbered 432 Massachusetts Avenue, corner of Walnut Street. It is supposed to be more than two hundred years old.

THE ABEL LOCKE HOUSE.

This is a fair type of the old houses of Arlington. It is on Massachusetts Avenue, corner of Forest Street, and bears up bravely under its weight of two hundred years.

Its next-door neighbor toward Lexington is the

WILLIAM LOCKE HOUSE.

Judging from its outward appearance, it must have been built at or before the time of the Abel Locke House.

THE CAPTAIN BENJAMIN LOCKE HOUSE.

Diagonally opposite the head of Forest Street, the "Old Lexington Road," now Appleton Street, leaves Massachusetts Avenue, passing over the hill to the west, but joins it again at no great distance. The second house, No. 7 Appleton Street, bears upon its chimney the date 1775. It is the Benjamin Locke House, which was built in 1726. In 1775 it was used as a Baptist meeting-house, having been bought for the purpose for the sum of one hundred dollars. It came into the possession of the Lockes later, and is now owned by them.

Farther on over the hill there stood till within a year another old Locke house. In fact, there were standing in this vicinity, and all at one time, no less than five old houses bearing the name of Locke, as I learn from a descendant, and all of whose occupants were more or less intimately connected with the stirring events of April 19, 1775.

> NEAR THIS SPOT
> SAMUEL WHITTEMORE
> THEN 80 YEARS OLD
> KILLED THREE BRITISH SOLDIERS
> APRIL 19, 1775.
> HE WAS SHOT, BAYONETED,
> BEATEN AND LEFT FOR DEAD,
> BUT RECOVERED AND LIVED
> TO BE 98 YEARS OF AGE.

The granite slab bearing the above inscription is on Mystic Street, in the rear of the Russell Schoolhouse.

If all the Revolutionary soldiers were of the same degree of toughness or equally tenacious of life, it is little wonder the British could not conquer them.

> THE SITE OF THE
> BLACK HORSE TAVERN
> COMMITTEE OF SAFETY
> IN 1775.

On the east side of Massachusetts Avenue, nearly opposite Linwood Street, stands a tablet with the above inscription.

> HERE STOOD COOPER'S TAVERN
> IN WHICH
> JABEZ WYMAN
> AND
> JASON WINSHIP
> WERE KILLED BY THE BRITISH
> APRIL 19, 1775.

A tablet with the above inscription is on Massachusetts Avenue, corner of Medford Street.

Arlington.

> AT THIS SPOT
> ON APRIL 19, 1775
> THE OLD MEN OF MENOTOMY
> CAPTURED A CONVOY OF
> EIGHTEEN SOLDIERS WITH SUPPLIES
> ON ITS WAY TO JOIN
> THE BRITISH AT LEXINGTON.

In front of the Unitarian Meeting-house on Massachusetts Avenue, near the center of the town, is to be seen a tablet with an inscription as above.

> SITE OF THE HOME OF
> JASON RUSSELL,
> WHERE HE AND ELEVEN OTHERS
> WERE CAPTURED,
> DISARMED AND KILLED
> BY THE RETREATING BRITISH
> ON APRIL 19, 1775.

On Massachusetts Avenue, near Jason Street, stands a stone tablet with the inscription as given above.

Lexington, like its sister, Concord, is so quiet and peaceful as to give to a stranger visiting the beautiful " Village Green " the impression that its gallantry on that memorable 19th of April, 1775, had given it henceforth a right to everlasting tranquillity. We have heard and read of hallowed ground! Here we see it and stand upon it, and feel like uncovering our heads as before some awe-inspiring presence.

Objects of historic interest are met on every hand. At the south end of the Common is a monument marking the site of three successive churches, the first built in 1714. Nearly opposite, on the Bedford road, stands the Buckman Tavern, from whose sides English bullets have been taken. Opposite, on the Concord road, is the house of Marrett and Nathan Monroe, built in 1729, and hence a witness of the battle. On the street north of the Green still stands the house of Jonathan Harrington with the following tablet:

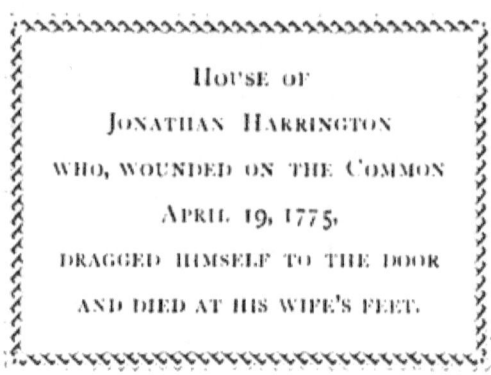

House of
Jonathan Harrington
who, wounded on the Common
April 19, 1775,
dragged himself to the door
and died at his wife's feet.

Lexington.

Every visitor notes the granite obelisk that marks the resting-place of the men of Lexington (and one from Woburn) who fell in the battle on the Common. It is on a rise of ground on the northwestern side of the battlefield.

> No British thirst of blood had they,
> No battle joy was theirs, who set
> Against the alien bayonet
> Their homespun breasts in that old day.
>
> . . . . . .
>
> They went where duty seemed to call;
> They scarcely asked the reason why;
> They only knew they could but die,
> And death was not the worst of all!
>
> WHITTIER.

THE OLD BOWLDER.

The inscription above embodies the words of Captain John Parker, as is affirmed to be probable by the Rev. Theodore Parker, his grandson.

"This bowlder, it is estimated, weighs from twelve to fifteen tons, and was drawn to the spot from a distance of two miles by a team of ten horses. It fitly symbolizes the firm, unyielding spirit of the men whose deed it commemorates," say the Lexington Historical Society in their interesting *Handbook to Lexington.*

> HOME OF JONATHAN HARRINGTON
> THE LAST SURVIVOR OF THE BATTLE
> OF LEXINGTON; BORN JULY 8, 1756;
> DIED MARCH 27, 1854.

The house marked by the above tablet is on Massachusetts Avenue, east side, about a mile from the Common in Lexington. "Young Harrington was the fifer boy of Captain Parker's company; only sixteen at the time of the battle."

On Massachusetts Avenue, corner of Pleasant Street, is a monument with the following inscription:

> NEAR THIS SPOT
> AT THE EARLY DAWN OF APRIL 19, 1775,
> BENJAMIN WELLINGTON, A MINUTE-MAN,
> WAS SURPRISED BY BRITISH SCOUTS AND DISARMED.
> WITH UNDAUNTED COURAGE HE BORROWED A GUN AND
> JOINED HIS COUNTRYMEN AT LEXINGTON GREEN.
> HE WAS THE FIRST ARMED MAN TAKEN IN THE REVOLUTION.
> HE FOUGHT AT SARATOGA AND WHITE PLAINS.

Lexington.

Toward the Common, and not far from the Munroe Tavern, is a tablet with the following inscription:

> On the hill to the south
> was planted
> one of the British field-pieces
> April 19, 1775,
> to command the village
> and its approaches,
> and near this place
> several buildings were burned.

One of the noticeable monuments of Lexington is about half a mile south of the Common, on Massachusetts Avenue. It represents a mounted field-piece cut in granite, and marks the spot where Earl Percy planted one to cover the retreat of the British troops.

MUNROE TAVERN.

This is a fair type of the Colonial houses of Lexington. The inscription on the tablet borne on its front is:

> EARL PERCY'S HEADQUARTERS
> AND HOSPITAL, APRIL 19, 1775.
> THE MUNROE TAVERN
> BUILT IN 1695.

South of this house and its next-door neighbor is the old Sanderson House. It received rough treatment at the hands of the retreating British, who added insult to injury by leaving one of their wounded to be cared for by the family on their return, they having fled at the approach of the enemy.

HANCOCK-CLARK HOUSE.

This house is on Hancock Street, about a third of a mile from the Common. The "L" part was built in 1698 or 1699, by the Rev. John Hancock, the second minister, and grandfather of John Hancock, governor of Massachusetts 1780-85 and 1787-93, Governor Hancock being the first signer of the Declaration of Independence. The Rev. Jonas Clark, the fourth minister, afterward owned the house, and here his thirteen children were born, all living to become men and women. The ministries of the Rev. John Hancock and the Rev. Jonas Clark in Lexington covered a period of one hundred and five years.

John Hancock and Samuel Adams were sleeping here on the night of the 18th of April, 1775, when awakened by Paul Revere. It is a shame that this house was removed, but a matter of thankfulness that it is preserved. In the autumn of 1896 it was moved across the street, and now stands on the northeast side of Hancock Street.

Lexington.

On Hancock Street, not far from the corner of Adams, is the Fiske House, which was at the time of the battle the home of Dr. Joseph Fiske, who became a surgeon in the Revolutionary army.

Farther on, toward Bedford, is the Lawrence House, a Colonial house, at one time occupied by the ancestors of the noted merchants, Amos and Abbott Lawrence.

All visitors to Lexington should find time to visit the Memorial Hall and Cary Library, as it contains objects of great historic interest and value. Chief among these, if we except the library of 13,000 volumes, is a painting of the battle of Lexington, by Sandham, which cost $4000.

Beyond the Common, on the Concord road, and about a mile out, is a tablet with the following inscription:

> AT THIS WELL
> APRIL 19, 1775,
> JAMES HAYWARD OF ACTON
> MET A BRITISH SOLDIER
> WHO, RAISING HIS GUN, SAID:
> "YOU ARE A DEAD MAN."
> "AND SO ARE YOU," REPLIED HAYWARD.
> BOTH FIRED, THE SOLDIER
> WAS INSTANTLY KILLED,
> AND HAYWARD MORTALLY WOUNDED.

Lexington.

On the retreat of the British from Concord, being hard pressed by the Americans, they made a stand on a hill "a mile and a half west of the Common." Here is a granite slab with the following inscription at the foot of the hill:

> THIS BLUFF
>
> WAS USED AS A RALLYING POINT
>
> BY THE BRITISH
>
> APRIL 19, 1775.
>
> AFTER A SHARP FIGHT
>
> THEY RETREATED TO FISKE HILL
>
> FROM WHICH THEY WERE DRIVEN
>
> IN GREAT CONFUSION.

This town is well worth visiting and knowing from its quiet natural beauties alone; but it becomes doubly interesting because it has been hallowed by historical events and literary associations, — because it was the dearly beloved home of the immortals, Emerson, Hawthorne, Thoreau, and the Alcotts.

The visitor seeking for historic sites and incidents naturally seeks first the

BATTLE GROUND.

It is on Monument Street, and not far from the Old Manse. The ground on which the British fought has a monument with the following inscription:

HERE
WAS MADE THE FIRST FORCIBLE RESISTANCE TO
BRITISH AGGRESSION.
ON THE OPPOSITE BANK STOOD THE AMERICAN MILITIA.
HERE STOOD THE INVADING ARMY.
AND ON THIS SPOT THE FIRST OF THE ENEMY FELL
IN THE WAR OF THE REVOLUTION,
WHICH GAVE INDEPENDENCE TO THESE UNITED STATES.
IN GRATITUDE TO GOD, AND IN THE LOVE OF FREEDOM,
THIS MONUMENT WAS ERECTED,
A.D. 1836.

THE BATTLE GROUND.

By the rude bridge that arched the flood,
  Their flag to April's breeze unfurled,
Here once the embattled farmers stood
  And fired the shot heard round the world.

. . . .

On this green bank, by this soft stream,
  We set to-day a votive stone
That memory may the deed redeem
  When, like our sires, our sons are gone.
                              EMERSON.

THE MINUTE-MAN.

This monument, full of spirit and earnestness, was designed by the famous sculptor of Concord, Mr. D. C. French. It stands on the side of the river, opposite to the spot on which the British fought, and marks the ground held by the Americans during the battle or a portion of it.

On the opposite side from the minute-man a stone in the wall marks the "Grave of British Soldiers."

> THE BRITISH TROOPS
> RETREATING FROM THE
> OLD NORTH BRIDGE
> WERE HERE ATTACKED IN FLANK
> BY THE MEN OF CONCORD
> AND NEIGHBORING TOWNS
> AND DRIVEN UNDER A HOT FIRE
> TO CHARLESTOWN.

This tablet stands at Merriam's Corner, past which the British were retreating on the road to Lexington.

THE OLD MANSE.

This house stands near the battleground, and the name, "Old Manse," the Scotch name for a country parsonage, is well applied, as it was built for the Rev. William Emerson, grandfather of Ralph Waldo Emerson, in 1765, and during most of its existence has been the home of ministers.

Mosses from an Old Manse inseparably connects Hawthorne's name with it, as he was at one time a resident of this house. It was a witness of the battle, and from one of its windows the widow of the Rev. William Emerson was a deeply interested observer of the same stirring event. All visitors to Concord should visit the Wayside, the real home of Hawthorne; the home of the Alcotts and the School of Philosophy,— all on the Lexington road, not far from Merriam's Corner; the Concord Antiquarian Society; the Public Library; and the different cemeteries, especially

Sleepy Hollow, and, time permitting, Walden Pond, the scene of the hermit life of a veritable child of Nature, Henry D. Thoreau.

In Sleepy Hollow the grave of Hawthorne is on the hill by Ridge Path; the grave of Thoreau is just behind; and a little farther on is the grave of R. W. Emerson, on the opposite side of Ridge Path. A great pine stands at the head of the grave, and a huge unhewn block of pink granite is his monument.

THE HOME OF EMERSON.

Probably no house in Concord, whether Colonial or more recent, is so eagerly sought out by visitors to this historic old town as is the simple house of the "Sage of Concord." Emerson lived here from 1835 till the time of his death, April 27, 1882. It may be of interest to the reader to be reminded that his death occurred only about one month after he had attended the funeral of his friend, Longfellow, who died March 24, 1882.

This house stands on the old road to Lexington, about equally distant from Merriam's Corner and the center of the town.

Bedford.

This town was incorporated under its present name in 1729, and is composed of territory formerly belonging to Concord, Billerica, and Cambridge.

As the visitor approaches the village of Bedford from the east on the main road, he sees on the right, and near the Common,

THE FIRST PARSONAGE,

or "Dominie Manse." It was built in 1729 by the Rev. Nicholas Bowes, whose wife, Lucy, was a daughter of the Rev. John Hancock, of Lexington.

Passing along the same road, past the Common, toward Concord, a second parsonage is reached, directly opposite a meeting-house, and known as

THE STEARNS HOUSE.

It has been the home of the Rev. Samuel Stearns (for forty years a minister here) and his descendants since 1796. It has just passed out of the family. It is worthy of mention that four descendants of the Rev. Samuel Stearns were ministers, the Rev. William A. Stearns being at one time president of Amherst College.

The next house north and on the same side of the road is also Colonial, built in 1756, and known as

THE JEREMIAH FITCH HOUSE.

Mr. Fitch was known as the "merchant."

Having seen the homes of the minister and the merchant, we are interested to find, on the same side of the road and next-door neighbor.

THE HOUSE OF THE SQUIRE,

one Mr. Stearns, a cousin of the Rev. Samuel Stearns. No finer specimen of Colonial house is to be found in New England, though probably it was built early in the present century.

Just here the road forks, one branch leading to Concord, the other to Billerica. At the "parting of the ways" stands the "Winthrop Oak," beneath whose branches met the men of Bedford and towns near by on the morning of April 19, 1775.

Some distance out on the Billerica branch is still to be seen an old

GARRISON HOUSE.

It was from a room in the upper story of this house that a brave young woman, unable to make the soldier on guard see a lurking Indian, seized a gun and shot him herself.

From the historian of Bedford, Mr. Abram English Brown, the writer was surprised to learn that *seventy-seven* men of the town were in the Concord fight. Fifty-two of them lie buried in the old cemetery near the Common. This cemetery well repays a visit. Among other quaint and curious things to be seen here is a bowlder bearing a tablet with the following inscription:

> CAMBRIDGE MOORE,
> CÆSAR PRESCOTT,
> CÆSAR JONES,
> NEGRO SLAVES, SOLDIERS
> IN THE REVOLUTION,
> 1775-1783.

Bedford.

Michael Bacon and his descendants have been among the most prominent of Bedford families since the settlement of the town.

THE BACON HOUSE

has been occupied by six generations of that name since its erection about 1682. It is on the hill on Mill Street, about a mile from its junction with Page Street. It is a large two-story house, facing the south, and commands a beautiful and extended prospect up and down the valley of the Shawshine.

On the opposite side of the street and a half-mile southward is to be seen one of the

PAGE HOUSES.

One of the family was a captain of minute-men and led in the fight at Concord bridge, April 19, 1775.

Among the historic relics of the town is the banner carried by the company on that day. The house is probably two hundred years old, but seems likely to last many more. One of the oldest of the Page houses has been recently removed and remodeled. It stands on Page Street, on the other side of the farm, which was once five hundred acres in extent. Page is, and always has been, an honored name in Bedford and Billerica. The old farm, much reduced in size, is now owned by descendants of the family of the eighth generation.

Opposite the place where Page Street crosses the Shawshine River is the

KENRICK HOUSE,

or tavern, Benjamin Danforth being the keeper at the time of the incorporation of the town, the house being commonly known as the

"SHAWSHINE."

It occupies the probable site of the Shawshine trading post of the time of King Philip. Its location at the head of navigation for canoes shows how wisely the spot was chosen to aid the Indians in bartering the products of the chase for the goods of the white man.

But of all the historic spots of Bedford and Billerica there is none that will have a more lasting interest than

THE BROTHER ROCKS,

located on the east bank of the Concord River, about two miles from Bedford Springs.

The following extract from John Winthrop's journal of April 24, 1638, will explain the origin of the name:

> "The Governour and Deputy [Dudley] went to Concord to view some land for farms, and, going down the river about four miles, they made choice of a place for one thousand acres for each of them. . . . At the place where the Deputy's land was to begin, there were two great stones, which they called The Two Brothers, in remembrance that they were brothers by their children's marriage and did so brotherly agree."

This interesting incident has been commemorated by "Winthrop-1638" on one of the rocks and "Dudley" on the other.

Billerica. 63

Not to know Billerica is to be ignorant of the most beautiful, healthful, and enterprising hill town of the Commonwealth. This is certainly the opinion of its residents, and the one who would contend for the contrary would need to be armed with stout arguments.

Her public library, the gift of an old resident, Mrs. Bennett, while stocked with choice books in goodly number, also contains a valuable collection of *historic bric-a-brac*, under the guardianship of the Billerica Historical Society.

This society is engaged at the present time in the praiseworthy work of designating by tablets in stone the historic houses and spots of the town. At North Billerica, easily seen from both the street and steam cars, is a massive bowlder with the following inscription:

```
BIRTHPLACE AND HOME OF

    ASA POLLARD,

FIRST TO FALL AT BUNKER HILL,

    JUNE 17, 1775.
```

Billerica.

Near the Billerica line, though in the town of Burlington, stands, in a very dilapidated and weatherworn condition,

THE AMOS WYMAN HOUSE.

It is the farmhouse, and is reached with about equal ease from Billerica and Woburn (formerly in the latter town) by the road connecting the towns, known as the " Boston " road. It is on a road at right angles with the " Boston " road, and about a mile from where the latter crosses the Shawshine.

The name of Wyman is, and has been, a prominent and honored one in Charlestown, Woburn, and Billerica for two hundred years, or since the arrival of the two brothers, John and Francis, who finally settled in Woburn in 1640. Amos was probably a son of one of these, and built the house that bears his name in 1666. The house stands upon an embankment buttressed by a stone wall, the top of which is reached by rude stone steps. In front of the embankment stand five giant buttonwoods that must have been planted soon after the house was built. At the southeast corner of the house is the well from which is drawn by the primitive " sweep " the most delicious water.

The present owner, who has lived in the house for the past seventy-one years, is Joshua Reed, born in the vicinity April 3, 1801. A bit of money placed in his palm gives one the "freedom of the house." A noticeable oddity is the peculiar construction of the cellar stairs. To parallel stringers of oak placed at the proper slant are fastened, with large wooden pins, *triangular* blocks of solid wood. This may have been common in the early days, but no similar case is known to us. Bits of fluted finish still cling about the front door, an indication that the builder was a person of means in his day.

Probably each particular town in the State has some peculiar excellence not possessed by the others, at least in the same degree. It is certainly true that the visitor to Lancaster is struck by the rich and varied beauty that Nature has bestowed upon the town. It is here that the north and the south branches unite to form the Nashua River; here are to be found a dozen or more ponds and lakes that nestle enchantingly among the hills; and here are her far-famed Intervales, of rich arable land; so that one readily sees the fitness of the common expression "Beautiful Lancaster."

The various attacks upon the town by the Indians, in 1675-6, under the instigation of the wily King Philip, are matters of history.

It is not so generally known, however, that in the last massacre and conflagration of February 9, 1776, only two buildings escaped,—the one a church, the other a house known as

THE JONATHAN LOCKE HOUSE.

It is now the residence of a gentleman by the name of Mr. N. C. Hawkins, who has owned and lived in it since 1859.

The owner takes commendable pride in the old house, and keeps it in excellent repair. "In old times there was a rope hanging from the rooftree and reaching to a well in the cellar, enabling the family to get water if besieged by an enemy."

THE ISAAC ROYALL HOUSE.

It was built by Colonel Isaac Royall, previously a West Indian merchant, in 1737, and was at the time considered one of the finest mansions in North America. He brought with him twenty-seven domestic slaves, for whose accommodation was erected a building of brick, now standing a little to the south of the mansion itself. During the siege of Boston it was the headquarters of General John Stark, of New Hampshire. It was also occupied for brief periods by General Sullivan and General Charles Lee, the latter giving it the name of "Hobgoblin Hall."

The builder lived to enjoy his beautiful home but two years. After the Revolution it was restored to his son, Isaac, who founded the first professorship of law at Harvard. The house is located on Main Street, corner of Royall, nearly a half-mile from the center of the city.

THE CRADOCK HOUSE.

It was so called from Matthew Cradock, first governor of the Massachusetts Company in New England, and was built in 1634. It is probably the first brick house built in the colony, and claims to be the oldest now standing in North America. Visitors should notice the circular portholes in the second story, as they will then more clearly understand the name of "The Old Fort," given it by the early inhabitants of "Mistick."

It is now the property of ex-Mayor Lawrence, who has shown much public spirit in restoring it to its primitive condition as regards its exterior. It is situated on Riverside Avenue, on the north side of the Mystic, and nearly midway between the cities of Medford and Malden.

On Grove Street, West Medford, on the celebrated Peter Chardon Brooks estate, is to be seen a brick wall, capped with slabs of freestone, which is about seventy feet in length, and is said to have been built by slaves more than two hundred years ago.

Not far from this wall is a noted black walnut tree twenty feet in circumference, and supposed to be four hundred years old.

Also within the grounds of Mr. Francis Brooks is to be seen a granite pillar with the following inscription:

To

SAGAMORE JOHN

AND THOSE MYSTIC

INDIANS WHOSE BONES

LIE HERE.

Sagamore John of Medford, Sagamore James of Lynn, and Sagamore George of Salem were sons of Sachem Nanephashemet.

At Medford Center stands a fine brick building bearing the name of Joseph Seccomb, and erected in 1756.

THE JONATHAN BROOKS HOUSE,

No. 2 Woburn Street, facing Rock Hill, is about two hundred years old, and may be easily distinguished by three fine sycamores in front.

A part of the house next to the above, No. 309 High Street, is equally old, and boasts the possession of a clock made in 1743. It keeps the time even now with surprising accuracy.

Winchester was formed chiefly of the territory formerly known as South Woburn, but includes some portions of West Cambridge (Arlington) and Medford.

The name was given in honor of William P. Winchester, a public-spirited citizen of Boston. The town was incorporated May 7, 1850.

Perhaps the most famous old house ever within its limits was

THE BLACK HORSE TAVERN.

It was built, in 1742, on Black Horse Hill, Maine Street, facing the Black Horse Terrace of to-day, and was standing as late as a dozen years ago, the march of improvement requiring its demolition. It was a rallying point for the minute-men, and they met here on the morning of the battle of Lexington.

It is worthy of remark that it was made a resting-place by Benjamin Thompson (Count Rumford) and his friend, Loammi Baldwin, during their long walk from North Woburn to Harvard to listen to the lectures of Professor Winthrop.

BROOKS HOUSE.

At Symmes' Corner was standing till recently the birthplace of John Brooks. It was built more than a hundred and seventy years ago. He was governor from 1816 to 1823. He did important military service in the Revolution, his most brilliant achievement being the storming and carrying of the German intrenchments at Saratoga.

Winchester has many interesting historic spots that will undoubtedly be marked by permanent tablets in the near future. One would like to see the site of Squaw Sachem's wigwam, corner of Church and Cambridge Streets, thus indicated. That of her husband, the powerful Nanephashemet (New Moon), was on Rock Hill, High Street, corner of Hasting's Lane, West Medford, and commanded a fine view of the Mystic. To describe adequately the natural beauties of Winchester would require many pages and a gifted pen.

Malden.

Malden is among the most wealthy and enterprising of our group of new cities, having increased in population more than tenfold since 1871.

It has at least one pre-Revolutionary house worthy of mention, which is commonly known as the

MISSIONARY HOUSE,

and is numbered 145 Main Street, corner of Wilson Avenue. It was built, about 1733, as a parsonage for the Rev. Joseph Emerson, but is especially distinguished as the birthplace of the Rev. Adoniram Judson, who was born August 9, 1788, and who was the first missionary from this country to Burmah.

He went to Burmah in 1813, translated the Bible into Burmese, and wrote a Burmese-English dictionary. He died at sea in 1850.

"How beautiful upon the mountains are the feet of him that bringeth good tidings, that publisheth peace."

The old house stands within ample grounds, and is quite embowered in trees, the most noticeable one being a magnificent specimen of buttonwood, or American sycamore.

BENJAMIN THOMPSON HOUSE.
(Count Rumford.)

This house, built in 1714 by Ebenezer Thompson, grandfather of the count, and now carefully preserved by a society formed for the purpose, is the birthplace of the famous Count Rumford, who was born here March 26, 1753. It is No. 90 Elm Street, North Woburn, adjacent to land occupied by the ancestors of ex-President Cleveland.

During a part of the war of the Revolution he fought against the Colonists. At the close of the war he entered the service of the King of Bavaria, from whom, on account of great service to the State, he received the title of Count of Rumford, the name Rumford formerly being the name of Concord, New Hampshire, where he at one time taught school. He deserves credit as an original scientific investigator and discoverer, and also as being one of the founders of the far-famed Royal Institution of Great Britain, having drawn up its original plan in 1799.

He gave five thousand dollars to the American Academy of Arts and Sciences, an equal sum to the Royal Society, London, and founded the Rumford professorship at Harvard. He died in 1814.

THE BALDWIN HOUSE.

Another Woburn house much sought for by visitors to this interesting town is that of Colonel Baldwin (now No. 12 Elm Street, North Woburn), a friend of Count Rumford, though he fought with the patriots at Lexington and during the siege of Boston. The house was built, in 1661, by Henry Baldwin, the great-grandfather of the colonel.

Colonel Baldwin was the engineer under whose supervision the Middlesex Canal was constructed, a portion of which is still to be seen on the Brooks estate, near Mystic Pond, West Medford. The Baldwin apple was named for the colonel.

Woburn was incorporated in 1642, and was previously known as "Charlestown Village."

Stoneham was a part of Charlestown, known as "Charlestown End," till 1725, when it was incorporated under its present name. Its first settler was Richard Holden, who removed to that part of Charlestown in 1640. A goodly number of his descendants are still living here and in the mother town.

Among the most interesting of its old houses is

THE JONATHAN GREEN HOUSE,

standing erect upon its "foot-square" oak sills during the summers and winters of nearly two hundred years. The old house, bereft of its ancient massive chimney, is still in the possession of the descendants of Richard Green. They have a tradition that slaves at one time performed the labor on the estate, which consisted of nearly five hundred acres and extended to Spot Pond.

It is numbered 37 Perkins Street, and is just across the line from the beautiful and picturesque Melrose Highlands.

> A SHARP FIGHT OCCURRED HERE
>
> BETWEEN THE PATRIOTS AND THE BRITISH
>
> APRIL 19, 1775.
>
> THIS MARKS BRITISH SOLDIERS' GRAVES.

The house in front of which this tablet stands was built by Timothy Tufts, and was a witness of the "sharp fight."

It is now (1897) the home of Mr. Timothy Tufts, grandson of the builder, and a genial old gentleman of seventy-eight years of age. It is on Elm Street, corner of Willow.

Somerville.

THE SAMUEL TUFTS HOUSE.

No one acquainted with the part that General Nathaniel Greene took in establishing the liberties of our country ever speaks or thinks of him without feelings of admiration second only to those felt for Washington himself.

This house, on Somerville Avenue, near Loring Street, was General Greene's headquarters during the siege of Boston. Past this house marched the British on their way to Lexington; the owner at the time, says *The Somerville Journal*, was in his kitchen running bullets.

The house is well preserved, but is not outwardly improved by the addition of modern chimney-tops.

On Sycamore Street, near the railroad crossing, stands, though recently removed a few rods from its old site for street improvement, the John Tufts House. During the siege of Boston it was the headquarters of General Charles Lee.

Southwest of this lies the most beautiful and famous Prospect Hill of Somerville, once called Mt. Pisgah. It is the site of the great earthwork built, by order of General Putnam, after the retreat from Bunker Hill.

Here, animated by a commendable public and patriotic spirit, the city has mounted several massive cannon on substantial iron carriages.

THE OLD POWDER HOUSE.

Near Tufts College, Somerville, is one of the most interesting relics of Colonial times to be met with in the Old Bay State.

It was built about the beginning of the eighteenth century by one John Mallet as a mill for grinding corn.

It became the property of the Massachusetts Bay Colony in 1747, and was used as a powder magazine till a more commodious one was built on Captain Patrick's Island,

Charles River, now a ruin, at the foot of Magazine Street, Cambridge.

The British, September 1, 1774, came here and seized two hundred and fifty half-barrels of powder. The legend (see Drake's *Landmarks of Middlesex*) takes one back to the time and home of Evangeline.

Soon after the battle of Bunker Hill a strong five-sided earthwork was made by the Americans on Winter Hill, to command the Mystic and the approach by land to Medford. It was under the command of General Sullivan.

General John Sullivan was born in Berwick, Maine, in 1740. He took part in the battles of Trenton and Princeton, and led the right wing of the army at the battle of Brandywine. He was afterward made attorney-general of New Hampshire, and was three times "president" of that State. His brother, James, also born in Berwick, was twice elected governor of Massachusetts.

On Main Street, opposite its junction with Broadway, is a tablet with the following inscription:

> PAUL REVERE
> PASSED OVER THIS ROAD ON HIS
> MIDNIGHT RIDE
> TO LEXINGTON AND CONCORD
> APRIL 18, 1775.
>
> SITE OF THE WINTER HILL FORT,
> A STRONGHOLD BUILT BY
> THE AMERICAN FORCES
> WHILE BESIEGING BOSTON
> 1775-6.

Somerville.

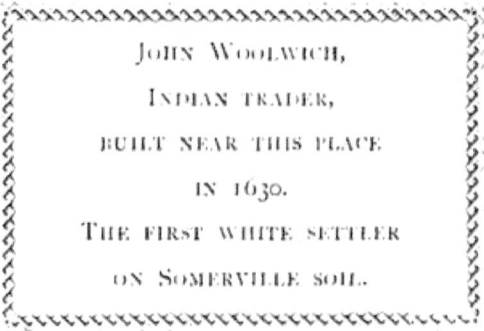

> JOHN WOOLWICH,
> INDIAN TRADER,
> BUILT NEAR THIS PLACE
> IN 1630.
> THE FIRST WHITE SETTLER
> ON SOMERVILLE SOIL.

This tablet is on Washington Street (the continuation of Kirkland Street, Cambridge), corner of Dane, not far from the boundary line between the cities of Somerville and Cambridge.

It would be interesting to know how many persons in New England are able to trace pleasing associations with the name of Boston to the early recollections of their childhood. We suspect the number is legion. Her history and traditions are so worthy and noble— so numerous are her deeds of patriotism and works of philanthropy— as to be sure to inspire in young minds sentiments of love and respect.

To know Boston well, — her educators, scholars, and statesmen, her benevolent institutions and her institutions of learning,— would be in itself a liberal education. It must needs be of no small interest, therefore, to know something of her infancy and childhood in a brief consideration of some of her most famous old buildings and historic spots.

> OPPOSITE THIS SPOT
> WAS SHED
> THE FIRST BLOOD
> OF THE AMERICAN REVOLUTION.

A tablet with the above inscription is to be seen on a building on State Street, corner of Exchange. "Opposite this spot" refers to the place of the Boston Massacre, March 5, 1770.

Directly opposite this tablet is the site of the first church in Boston, the first minister being the Rev. John Wilson, the very man whose harangue from the branches of an old oak on Cambridge Common decided an election for governor against Henry Vane and in favor of John Winthrop. This first church was built in 1632, and was a rude structure of logs with a thatched roof.

Dorchester Heights, South Boston, now Telegraph Hill, has upon it a granite monument telling that on this ridge Washington placed the batteries that drove the British from Boston. Dorchester Heights was a part of the town of Dorchester till 1804.

THE OLD SOUTH CHURCH.

THE OLD SOUTH CHURCH.

The affectionate regard in which this venerable meetinghouse is held extends much beyond the limits of Boston. It was built in 1729 on its present site, Washington Street, corner of Milk. It was for a long time the rallying point for patriots in times of political excitement, and for the discussion of questions of moment to the Colony. It was here that the "Indians" donned their fantastic suits preparatory to emptying the tea into the harbor. The British, during the Revolutionary War, used it for cavalry drill and exercise, thus causing Washington to remark that he could not understand the reverence of the British for their own churches when they so readily desecrated this.

The church was bought of the owners, by the Old South Preservation Society, for $430,000, and is now a rich museum of historic relics.

THE OLD STATE HOUSE.

Where the Old State House now stands stood the Town House of 1657. This was succeeded in 1713 by a State House, and this in turn by the present building, erected in 1748, at the head of State Street. Directly in front of the eastern end of the building the Boston Massacre took place, March 5, 1770.

"Here," says John Adams, "Independence was born."

And it was here that the patriots, Samuel and John Adams, James Otis, and Joseph Warren contended against British oppression with a zeal and stoutness of heart born of the profoundest conviction.

It is now a museum in charge of the Bostonian Society, and contains two thousand or more historic objects of great interest and value to the student of Colonial times.

FANEUIL HALL.

FANEUIL HALL.

Peter Faneuil, a descendant of the Huguenots, was born at New Rochelle, New York, in 1700, and died in Boston at the age of forty-three years.

"He possessed a large estate, and employed it in doing good."

Faneuil Hall, the "Cradle of Liberty," was built by him and presented to the city of Boston for a market and public hall, the hall to be for the perpetual use of the people free of charge.

If it be the object of a monument to perpetuate the memory, how excellent is the one Peter Faneuil erected to himself in the noble building that bears his name!

The original building was finished in 1743, but, being burnt, was rebuilt in 1763, the dedicatory oration being delivered by James Otis. In 1806 it was greatly enlarged under the direction of the celebrated architect, Bulfinch.

Its walls have resounded to more genuine eloquence than those of any other building in Boston, for here have spoken the Adamses, Otis, Warren, Webster, and a host of others. To look upon the works of art that adorn its walls is in itself an inspiration, for here are to be seen portraits of Washington, Knox, Hancock, the Adamses, Governor Andrew, General Warren, Faneuil, Lincoln, Everett, Commodore Preble, and Webster in the act of replying to Hayne in the United States' Senate.

It is between North and South Market Streets.

HOUSE OF PAUL REVERE.

In North Square there is now standing an old house of the "overhang" pattern, having on its front a tablet with the following inscription :

> HERE LIVED
> PAUL REVERE
> 1770–1800.
> PLACED BY
> PAUL REVERE CHAPTER
> DAUGHTERS OF THE AMERICAN REVOLUTION.

The house in which he was born, January 1, 1735, stood on Hanover (then North), opposite Clark Street, near the corner of Tileston. He was the son of Paul and Deborah (Hitchborn) Revere, descendants of a noble Huguenot family, and was the third of twelve children. He learned of his father the art of working in silver and gold, and taught himself to engrave on copper, money for the Provincial Congress being printed from plates engraved by him.

He also established a foundry for casting bells and cannon in Boston and a copper rolling mill in Canton, Massachusetts, still bearing his name. He was educated at the North Grammar School, North Bennett Street, with which school John Tileston was connected as pupil, teacher, and master for eighty years. His place of worship was chiefly the "New Brick Church," commonly known as the "Cockerel Church," the site of which is now occupied by the Boston Seaman's Friend Society building, numbered 287 Hanover Street, nearly opposite Parmenter. After a service of one hundred and forty-eight years on the spire of the New Brick Church, the "cockerel," made by Deacon Shem Drowne, is still doing duty as a weather-vane from the lofty spire of the Shepard Memorial Church, Cambridge. Paul Revere was a staunch patriot, one of the Boston "Tea Party," whose memory is perpetuated in the Revere House, Boston, in the town of Revere, formerly North Chelsea, but in no way more lastingly than in "The Midnight Ride of Paul Revere," by Longfellow.

KING'S CHAPEL.

This historic old church stands on Tremont Street, corner of School, and was the first Episcopal Church in New England. It was here that Oliver Wendell Holmes worshiped for the most part, and of it he speaks in words of affection. It is now a Unitarian Church.

THE OLD NORTH CHURCH.

The building was torn down by the British in 1775. It fronted North Square, about which there lived in Colonial times several aristocratic families.

CHRIST CHURCH.

This church, the "Old North Church" of Longfellow's poem, is on Salem Street, opposite Hull, and was built in 1723. From the tower of this church General Gage witnessed the battle of Bunker Hill. Tablets with the following inscriptions are to be seen upon its front:

    CHRIST CHURCH,
        1723.

    THE SIGNAL LANTERNS OF
           PAUL REVERE
    DISPLAYED IN THE STEEPLE OF THIS CHURCH
         APRIL 18, 1775,
    WARNED THE COUNTRY OF THE MARCH
       OF THE BRITISH TROOPS TO
      LEXINGTON AND CONCORD.

THE OLD CORNER BOOKSTORE.

On Washington Street, corner of School, is the Old Corner Bookstore, erected in 1712, and said to be the oldest brick building in Boston.

On its site there once stood the house of Anne Hutchinson. She was banished from Massachusetts in 1637 because of her religious views. She was killed in New York by the Indians in 1643.

This building has been a bookstore since 1828, and is worthy of mention, if for no other reason, as the literary headquarters of our own most famous authors, Longfellow, Holmes, Whittier, Lowell, and Emerson, as well as of those visiting Boston from abroad.

The site of the house of John Hancock, built in 1737 by his uncle, Thomas Hancock, and demolished in 1863, is on Beacon Street, a little west of the present State House, and is marked by a tablet.

The Somerset Club House, 42 Beacon Street, occupies the site of the house once owned by the great artist, John Singleton Copley, where his son, of the same name (afterwards celebrated as Lord Lyndhurst, of England), was born.

Dorchester.

THE PIERCE HOUSE.

This house, built in 1635, has always been occupied by persons of the name of Pierce. It is also unique in another respect: its sides are lined with seaweed, as a better protection against the arrows of the Indians, according to one authority. We suspect, however, if the whole truth were known, a desire for protection against the shafts of old Boreas might have had something to do with it. This house stands on Oak Avenue. On Washington Street stands the Barnard-Capen House, a portion of which was built in 1632. The Blake House was built in 1640, and is near Five Corners.

THE EVERETT HOUSE.

Edward Everett, the eloquent and finished orator, the profound scholar, the great statesman, seems to be of our own time and generation; yet he was born in 1794, in Dorchester, in a house built about 1770 by his father, the Rev. Oliver Everett, and which stands on the corner of Boston and Pond Streets.

He was professor of Greek at Harvard College 1819–25, editor of the *North American Review* 1819–24, member of Congress 1825–35, governor of Massachusetts 1836–40, minister to England 1841–5, president of Harvard College 1846–9, and Secretary of State 1852–3.

His *Orations and Speeches* are published in four volumes. It is remarkable that Edward should have attained to such fame and eminence as to completely overshadow his older brother, Alexander, who, born in 1792, entered Harvard

College in 1802, in the *eleventh* year of his age, and, although the youngest in his class, he was graduated with the highest honors. He was a noted man of letters, and occupied many important positions under the government of the United States.

THE VOSE HOUSE.

("THE BIRTHPLACE OF AMERICAN LIBERTY.")

The following inscription is now to be seen on a tablet on the Vose House. For a full text of the "Suffolk Resolves" see *Life and Times of Joseph Warren*, by Richard Frothingham. These Resolves were taken to the Continental Congress in Philadelphia by Paul Revere.

This interesting old house is near the bridge at Milton Lower Mills, on Adams Street, and is noticeable for the stately English elms (six in number) that surround and tower above it as if in perpetual guardianship.

> IN THIS MANSION ON THE 9TH OF SEPT. 1774, AT A
> MEETING OF THE DELEGATES OF EVERY TOWN AND
> DISTRICT IN THE COUNTY OF SUFFOLK, THE MEMORA-
> BLE SUFFOLK RESOLVES WERE ADOPTED. THEY WERE
> REPORTED BY MAJ.-GEN. JOSEPH WARREN, WHO FELL
> IN THEIR DEFENCE, IN THE BATTLE OF BUNKER HILL,
> JUNE 17, 1775. THEY WERE APPROVED BY THE MEM-
> BERS OF THE CONTINENTAL CONGRESS, AT CARPEN-
> TERS HALL, PHILADELPHIA, ON 17, SEPT., 1774. THE
> RESOLVES TO WHICH THE IMMORTAL PATRIOT HERE
> FIRST GAVE UTTERANCE, AND THE HEROIC DEEDS OF
> THAT EVENTFUL DAY ON WHICH HE FELL, LED THE
> WAY TO AMERICAN INDEPENDENCE. POSTERITY WILL
> ACKNOWLEDGE THAT VIRTUE WHICH PRESERVED THEM
> FREE AND HAPPY.

But we must not stop with the Vose House, for the beautiful town of Milton can show several others of interest.

Following Adams Street to the summit of Milton Hill, there appears to glad eyes a vision of grandeur and beauty that must be to residents "a joy forever." The point of view is eighty feet above the Neponset, whose broad estuary extends to the bay, where one sees the shipping, the islands, and the lighthouses of Boston's fine harbor.

This inspiring view was commanded by the summer residence of Governor Thomas Hutchinson, replaced some twenty-five years ago by a modern house standing on the exact site of the old mansion, Adams Street, corner of Hutchinson.

The old farmhouse and barn, built in 1743, are, however, still standing. The estate consisted originally of several hundred acres extending on the north and east to the Neponset. This place is the chief scene of *The Governor's Garden*, by George R. R. Rivers, and is now owned by the heirs of the late Lydia C. Russell.

Thomas Hutchinson was born in Boston in 1711, and was governor from 1771 to 1774. He was the author of a *History of the Colony of Massachusetts Bay*, inherited large wealth from his father, and refused to live in the "ancient abode of the royal governors," the Province House, on the ground that he had a better one of his own in North Square.

THE TUCKER HOUSE,

near Brush Hill Turnpike, is of interest because of the prominence of its owner, Dr. Tucker, a surgeon in the Revolution. It is said to have been built in 1750.

Roxbury.

It has been said that Boston might well challenge almost any city in the world as to the beauty of her suburban towns and cities. Roxbury could easily claim to be among the first of these in picturesqueness.

The town became a city in 1846, and was annexed to Boston in 1867. During the Revolutionary and later wars the town furnished her full quota of both officers and men, the most prominent of the former being Generals Dearborn, Heath, and Joseph Warren.

Probably more young hearts have been made to throb with patriotic emotions by stories of the life and character of Joseph Warren than by those of any other native of the Commonwealth.

The house in which he was born is not now standing, but its site is marked by a substantial memorial house of Roxbury puddingstone trimmed with granite. Its location is 130 Warren Street, a short distance above Dudley Street.

On the left of the front entrance is a tablet bearing the following inscription:

> ON THIS SPOT STOOD A HOUSE, ERECTED IN
> 1720 BY JOSEPH WARREN OF BOSTON,
> REMARKABLE FOR BEING THE BIRTHPLACE
> OF GENERAL JOSEPH WARREN,
> HIS GRANDSON, WHO WAS KILLED ON
> BUNKER HILL, JUNE 17, 1775.

On the right, another with the following:

> JOHN WARREN, A DISTINGUISHED PHYSICIAN
> AND ANATOMIST, WAS ALSO BORN HERE.
> THE ORIGINAL MANSION BEING IN RUINS,
> THIS HOUSE WAS BUILT BY JOHN C. WARREN, M.D.,
> IN 1846, SON OF THE LAST NAMED, AS A
> PERMANENT MEMORIAL OF THIS SPOT.

Roxbury.

The beautiful and conspicuous Cochituate stand-pipe, on Fort Avenue, near Highland Street, stands on the site of one of the strongest forts built by the patriots during the siege of Boston.

This site was, with one exception, the highest point of land in Roxbury. The spot is further marked by a granite monument bearing the following inscription :

> ON THIS EMINENCE STOOD
> ROXBURY HIGH FORT,
> A STRONG EARTHWORK, PLANNED BY
> HENRY KNOX AND JOSEPH WATERS
> AND ERECTED BY THE AMERICAN ARMY
> JUNE, 1775 — CROWNING THE FAMOUS
> ROXBURY LINES OF INVESTMENT.
>
> THE SIEGE OF BOSTON.

Roxbury High Fort commanded the Neck and also the road to Dedham, the depot of military supplies.

"Jamaica Plain," says Francis S. Drake, "is one of the loveliest spots in New England."

It, being a part of West Roxbury, was set off from Roxbury in 1852, and with it is now a part of Boston. One of the most interesting old houses here is

THE LORING HOUSE.

It is a two-story house, with porticos on three sides supported by fluted columns, and, with its ample and well-kept grounds, presents a most pleasing appearance. It is opposite the intersection of Centre and South Streets, directly opposite the Soldiers' Monument.

In May, 1775, it was the headquarters of General Greene. It is now known as the Greenough Mansion.

Loring was born in Roxbury, held the king's commission as commodore, and did most active and efficient service, being at the capture of Quebec with General Wolfe.

THE HALLOWELL HOUSE.

The Hallowell House is on Centre Street, corner of Boylston, and bears upon one of its chimneys its name and the date, 1738. During the siege of Boston this house was taken possession of by the patriots and used as a hospital for the soldiers in camp at Roxbury.

This, coupled with the fact that he held office under the crown, leads one to infer that he was a Tory.

Visitors to this old house, which seems to have been changed somewhat in recent years, will be pleased to notice the fine buttonwoods that stand in the sidewalk in front of the estate.

THE OLD FAIRBANKS HOUSE.

We believe Dedham may well claim the possession of the quaintest old "lean-to" within the Commonwealth. The main house was built in 1636, the year of the founding of Harvard College, by John Fairbanks, who came the previous year from Somerby, England, bringing with him some portions of the framework now in the house. The east wing was built to accommodate his son John, who was married in 1641.

The house has always been the residence of some member of the Fairbanks family, its present occupant being a maiden lady of the eighth generation.

In the "best" room is a fine oil painting of Prudence Fairbanks at the age of ninety years, she being of the seventh generation. The inventor of the celebrated Fairbanks scales was Thaddeus, who, having been knighted by the Austrian emperor, was ever after known as Sir Thaddeus.

In one of the chambers the visitor is shown utensils that suggest with emphasis primitive times in the Colony. Among these may be mentioned an ox saddle, reminding one of Priscilla, the Puritan maiden, as "through the Plymouth woods passed onward the bridal procession"; also a wicker pannier, an ancient chafing dish, a frying pan with handle four feet in length, a flintlock musket six feet in length, and old Dutch tiles with figures in blue, — a sight to make one "green with envy."

The house is on East Street, corner of Eastern Avenue. In the front wall is a tablet with the following inscription:

> HOMESTEAD OF
> JONATHAN FAIRBANKS,
> WHO, WITH HIS SONS,
> JOHN, GEORGE, AND JONATHAN, JR.,
> SIGNED THE
> DEDHAM COVENANT
> SEPT. 10, O. S. 1636.

THE ADAMS HOUSES.

About half a mile from the center of Quincy, in a southerly direction, on the old Plymouth road, here called Hancock Street, stand the quaint old Adams Houses, the one at the right being the birthplace of John Adams; the other, built in 1716, as is inferred from that date on a brick in the old chimney, is the birthplace of his son, John Quincy Adams.

The former is in the care of the Daughters of the Revolution and the latter, of the Quincy Historical Society.

Both these houses have inner walls, the one of burnt, the other of unburnt brick, and both are unique (so far as I know) in having *no boards* on the outer walls — merely clapboards fastened directly to the studding with, of course, wrought-iron nails.

The people of Quincy (a part of Braintree till 1792) take a justifiable pride in the fact that their town is the birthplace of John Hancock as well as of the Adamses.

Their admiration for the Adamses is shown in the commemorative tablets on each side of the pulpit in the Unitarian Church, bearing testimony to their fidelity, patriotism, and sterling character in words of highest eulogium. The remains of both the Adamses and their wives lie buried beneath the massive stone walls of this church.

Hingham.

Hingham (first called "Bare Cove," as indicated by its town seal) was probably settled soon after Plymouth, as the first church was erected in 1635.

The present one, on Main Street, near Derby Academy, called the "Old Ship," was built in 1681 of large timber hewn from white oak logs, even the smaller ones showing plainly the marks of the "broadaxe." It claims the remarkable distinction of being the oldest church in the United States now in use as a place of worship.

New and comfortable pews have taken the place of the old ones, but the ancient sounding-board is still here, and a part of the wood of the old pulpit remains. The roof of the old church being a four-sided pitch roof, the bell tower stands exactly over the center, which necessitates the ringing of the bell from within one of the pews.

At first the bell ringer stood *above*, and, that he might know when the minister came, an opening through the ceiling, covered by a pane of glass, commanded a view of the pulpit.

LINCOLN HOUSE.

Probably the most famous dwelling house in Hingham is the birthplace of General Benjamin Lincoln. It stands at the center of the town, on North Street, corner of Lincoln. It is known to be a very old house, though the date of its erection cannot be ascertained. It has a decidedly well-to-do air about it, which, with its pleasant location, makes a picture one does not easily tire of looking at.

General Lincoln was born in 1733 and died in 1810. He held high command under Washington, and was wounded at Bemis Heights in 1777. He was put in command of the army of the South, and, although unsuccessful at Savannah and obliged to surrender the city of Charleston, S. C., he continued to hold the respect of Washington, who appointed him to receive the sword of Cornwallis at Yorktown. The United States has upon its roll of honor few names that shine with a more enduring luster than that of Lincoln.

On the same street and next door is the Solomon Lincoln House, built before 1747.

On South Street, corner of Central, is the

THAXTER HOUSE,

very venerable in appearance, probably built about 1700. It is overshadowed by a symmetrical elm that must have belonged to the "forest primeval."

Sudbury.

THE WAYSIDE INN.

In Sudbury, about a mile from the Wayside Inn Station, on the Massachusetts Central Railroad, or three miles from Sudbury Village, stands to-day, in a good state of preservation, the Wayside Inn immortalized by the pen of Longfellow.

It is two hundred and ten years old, and has been used for the greater part of its existence as a tavern under the name of the Red Horse. The proprietor has always been some member of the Howe family. It claims the high honor of having had both Washington and Lafayette as guests.

The chief incentive, however, to pilgrimages to this staunch, oak-framed old tavern is, and doubtless will continue to be, the fact that the poet Longfellow made it the scene of his "Tales of a Wayside Inn," whose characters, I am told, are the following :

LANDLORD	LYMAN HOWE.
STUDENT	HENRY WARE WALES.
JEW	ISAAC EDRAELES.
SICILIAN	LUIGI MONTI.
MUSICIAN	OLE BULL.
POET	THOMAS W. PARSONS.
THEOLOGIAN	PROF. TREADWELL, or REV. SAMUEL LONGFELLOW.

"As ancient is the hostelry
As any in the land may be,
Built in the old Colonial day,
When men lived in a grander way
With ampler hospitality;
A kind of old Hobgoblin Hall
Now somewhat fallen to decay,
With weather stains upon the wall,
And stairways worn and crazy doors,
And creaking and uneven floors,
And chimneys huge and tiled and tall.
. . . .
A region it seems,
A place of slumber and of dreams,
Remote among the wooded hills!
. . . .
Night and day the panting teams
Stop under the great oaks that throw
Tangles of light and shade below
On roofs and doors and window-sills."
. . . .

> CAPTAIN SAMUEL WADSWORTH
> OF MILTON, HIS LIEUTENANT SHARP OF
> BROOKLINE, CAPTAIN BROCLEBANK
> OF ROWLEY, WITH ABOUT 26 OTHER
> SOULDIERS, FIGHTING FOR THE
> DEFENCE OF THEIR COUNTRY, WERE
> SLAIN BY YE INDIAN ENEMY,
> APRIL 18TH, 1676, LYE BURIED
> IN THIS PLACE.

Captain Wadsworth and his men were drawn into an ambush near South Sudbury, at a place called Green Hill, where the tablet now stands. It was erected by President Wadsworth, of Harvard College, a son of the ill-fated captain.

THE WALKER GARRISON HOUSE.

Since about 1660 this house, a two-story "lean-to," has stood a silent witness to the deadly enmity then, and for a long time after, existing between the white man and the Indian in the Colony; for it was built as a place of safety for the people in King Philip's War, its walls being made of solid oak plank four inches in thickness.

This interesting old house is in the westerly part of the town, very near the Massachusetts Central Railroad, and about one-fourth of a mile from the Wayside Inn Station.

THE BROWN HOUSE.

About a mile from Watertown Center, on Main Street, near Hersom, is the old Brown House, certainly the most venerable looking and probably the oldest in Watertown. There seems to be evidence that it was built in 1633. It is now and always has been occupied by families by the name of Brown. Its inner walls are of brick.

COCHRANE HOUSE.

On the river road, better known as the old Waltham road, stands the Cochrane House, built about 1725, to which some of the wounded at the Concord fight were taken.

Watertown.

The Coolidge Tavern of the Revolutionary times, now known as the Brigham House, is the first on the left (No. 40 Galen Street) in crossing the bridge from Watertown toward Newton. It had the high honor of furnishing lodging on one occasion to the first president of the United States, while making a tour of New England in 1789.

> THIS STONE MARKS THE SITE
> OF THE DWELLING HOUSE IN
> WHICH GENERAL WARREN SLEPT
> THE NIGHT BEFORE THE BATTLE
> OF BUNKER HILL.

The house that formerly stood here was known as the Marshall Fowle House, and is now standing at 14 Marshall Street. It formerly stood, as the tablet indicates, on Mt. Auburn Street, corner of Marshall.

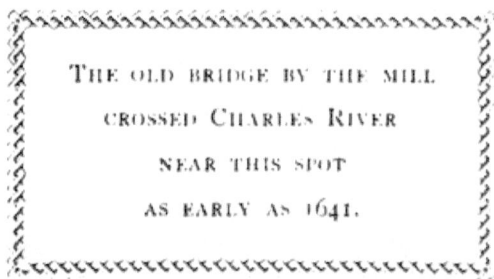

> THE OLD BRIDGE BY THE MILL
> CROSSED CHARLES RIVER
> NEAR THIS SPOT
> AS EARLY AS 1641.

This tablet stands on the bridge over the Charles at Watertown.

On the left bank of the Charles River, where Stony Brook joins it, stands Norembega Tower, a picturesque and massive stone structure erected at great expense by Professor Eben Norton Horsford to mark the site of the city of Norembega. The top of the tower (reached by a circular stone stairway) commands a fine view of a portion of the Charles River valley.

Nothing could give more striking evidence of strong conviction of the truth of his conclusions respecting the location of the "Lost Norembega" than the expenditure of money in the erection of this tower.

Upon its base are elaborate tablets appropriately inscribed.

Since the death of her father Miss Cornelia Horsford, with praiseworthy zeal, is continuing investigations to establish beyond a doubt, if possible, the truth of the positions so stoutly defended by him. A remarkable stone recently discovered by her in the town of Weston, and bearing Runic inscriptions, is a possible link in the chain of evidence leading thereto.

Chelsea.

THE GOVERNOR BELLINGHAM MANSION.

This is certainly as fine a specimen of a Colonial house as one meets with in many a day's travel, and bears with dignity the name of mansion. It was undoubtedly the summer residence of Governor Richard Bellingham, as he also had a very substantial house in Boston, near Pemberton Square. He came here from England in 1634, and became one of the wealthiest and most extensive landholders of the chartered company. In 1641 he became Governor, serving ten years in that capacity, and thirteen as Deputy-Governor.

He was twice married, performing in the second instance the marriage ceremony himself. For this he was prosecuted, but escaped by refusing to leave the bench, "thus officiating at his own trial."

His sister was executed as a witch in 1656, being the second victim in America of that "absurd fanaticism." A writer of the time says "She was hanged for having more wit than her neighbors." The Bellingham House is 34 Parker Street, "Caryville." In this old house, built about 1670, the writer finds a feature that he had often read about and heard of but had never before seen, — a secret passage connecting the cellar with a secret chamber in the attic ! About 1749 a gentleman by the name of Carey married a Bellingham, since which time the house has been more commonly known as the Carey Mansion.

THE PRATT HOUSE.

In all our searches for famous old country houses, rarely, if ever, have we found one more satisfying to the eye than is this, built, it is supposed, about 1660. It is a somewhat rare combination of the "gambrel roof" and the "lean-to," and is pleasing as a whole and also when studied in detail. It is numbered 481 Washington Avenue.

It was in this house that Increase Mather, — born in Dorchester in 1639, President of Harvard College, 1684–1701, and pastor of the North Church, Boston, for sixty-two years, — took refuge from the persecutions of Governor Andros. He finally escaped to England, where he obtained a new charter for the Colony. It may be supposed that his escape to a vessel in the harbor was made easy by the close proximity of "Snake River," that has its rise almost at the very door of the house. The house has always been occupied by some member of the Pratt family, the present representative being "aunt Rebeckah." She is a *real* "Daughter of the Revolution," her father being a boy in the army and afterward a Revolutionary pensioner.

In 1727 the family purchased in Boston a slave by the name of "Jack Langdon." The room under the "lean-to" where he died is pointed out to the visitor.

In a wall about Washington Park, Prattville, is a stone with an inscription marking the Barrack Grounds of Colonel Gerrish. The stone was a doorstep to a Pratt house not now standing.

Salem.

The city of Salem is one of the most interesting old cities of the Commonwealth of Massachusetts, apart from its objects and places of historic interest. Its citizens take a justifiable pride in the fame of her great men, both native and adopted.

Among her favorite native citizens may be mentioned Nathaniel Bowditch, born in 1773, a profound mathematician and translator of the *Mécanique Celeste* of Laplace; William H. Prescott, the historian, born in 1796; Professor Benjamin Pierce, of Harvard University, one of the greatest mathematicians of any age; Nathaniel Hawthorne, born in 1804, July 4, at 27 Union Street; John Rogers, born in 1829, corner of Washington and Lynde Streets, a famous sculptor, noted for his groups or statuettes.

Among Salem's adopted sons may be mentioned Judge Joseph Story (his son, W. W. Story, the sculptor, was born here, 26 Winter Street, in 1819), Benjamin Thompson (Count Rumford), and General James Miller, author of " I will Try, Sir " at Lundy's Lane.

All visitors to Salem, if they have an hour at their disposal, should visit the Peabody Museum and the Essex Institute, the pride of her citizens and evidences of their public spirit.

Here are to be seen, " without money and without price," not only a rich collection of historic bric-à-brac and curios from foreign lands (Salem being at one time the seat of the East India trade), but noteworthy collections of the local fauna, most conveniently arranged for study and comparison, together with specimen minerals and Indian stone implements without number.

WARD HOUSE.

A good type of the old houses of Salem is the Ward House, built about 1684. It is near the foot of St. Peter Street, and is remarkable for its second story "overhang."

At 71 Essex Street is the Narbonne House, noticeable for its "lean-to." It was built about 1680, and well represents the houses of that time.

The house numbered 138 Federal Street was built in 1782, and has the honor of having given entertainment to both Washington and Lafayette.

THE OLD FIRST CHURCH.

This church is said to have been originally a tavern, standing well out in the road to Lynn. It was afterwards removed to Washington, corner of Essex Street, and used as a church.

It still has its original framework, but its preservation has required a new exterior covering. It is now a much visited and honored relic, and stands in the rear grounds of the Essex Institute.

Its extreme smallness is a surprise to the visitor, as is also a gallery that could have been reached only by means of a ladder.

Salem.

> IN THE REVOLUTION
> THE FIRST ARMED RESISTANCE
> TO THE ROYAL AUTHORITY
> WAS MADE AT THIS BRIDGE,
> 26 FEB., 1775,
> BY THE PEOPLE OF SALEM.
> THE ADVANCE OF 300
> BRITISH TROOPS, LED BY
> LIEUT.-COL. LESLIE AND SENT BY
> GEN. GAGE TO SEIZE
> MUNITIONS OF WAR, WAS
> HERE ARRESTED.

The above tablet stands at the Old North Bridge, which crosses North River at the foot of North Street.

THE ROGER WILLIAMS HOUSE.

This quaint old house is said to have been built in 1634, thus disputing with the Cradock House, Medford, the honor of being the oldest now standing in North America.

It was from this house that the persecution of the General Court at Boston drove Roger Williams in 1636 to become the founder of the State of Rhode Island.

It is sometimes known as the "Witch House," because trials for witchcraft were begun here. It now stands, as always, on the corner of Essex and North Streets.

THE GEORGE CABOT HOUSE.

This house, 104 Cabot Street, though more than a hundred years old, has an air that indicates a period more modern.

Beverly was at one time the home of three brothers Cabot, — Andrew, John, and George, — the last, the great-grandfather of Henry Cabot Lodge, being the most famous. He was at one time a representative to the Massachusetts Provincial Congress (1776), and also a senator in Congress, and was offered the Secretaryship of the Navy by John Adams. He was also president of the famous Hartford Convention, December, 1814.

At this house in October, 1789, George Cabot entertained Washington at breakfast.

"SUNDAY SCHOOL" HOUSE.

On Front Street, corner of Davis, stands a modest and unpretending old house, in which the people of Beverly take no inconsiderable pride, since it lays claim to having furnished accommodations to the first Sunday school assembled in America.

It is a matter of regret that implicit reliance cannot be placed on all the various claims of "first" and "oldest" that are put forth, since about six different towns in the Commonwealth lay claim to the possession of the "oldest house" now standing in America.

Robert Raikes, of Gloucester, England, was the founder of Sunday schools in 1781, and it is quite probable that Beverly has good ground for the claim that she makes in this instance.

THE REBECCA NOURSE HOUSE.

Danvers was set off from Salem in 1752; a part of this division became South Danvers in 1855, and this, in turn, became Peabody in 1868. Still, Danvers is a good-sized and beautiful town, made up of Tapleyville, Danvers Plains, and Danversport. Probably there is no town of its size in the Commonwealth that has more houses of Colonial time now standing than has the town of Danvers. A good type of these is the Nourse House, built in 1636 by Townsend Bishop, and now standing in a field west of Pine Street, near Tapleyville. It takes its name from the good woman who lived in it at the time of her martyrdom to the witchcraft delusion, then prevalent in both the Old World and the New. A monument to her memory has recently been erected among the "Pines," not far from the house.

On Sylvan Street, corner of Collins, stands the "Lindens," built by Robert Hooper in 1750, which was the headquarters of General Gage in 1774. It is one of the most beautiful "mansions" of Colonial times, and is now the home of Mr. Francis Peabody.

On Maple Street, near Newbury, stands the house in which General Israel Putnam was born.

On the corner of Elm and High Streets stands the Page House, in which General Gage had a private office. The Houlton House, built in 1650, in which Judge Samuel Houlton, a noted statesman, was born in 1738, stands at the corner of Houlton and Centre Streets. Well out in a field off Water Street is the George Jacobs House, in which have lived ten generations of that name. George Jacobs himself was hanged as a wizard in 1692.

No visitor to Danvers would willingly omit seeing the house built about 1675 by a son of Governor Endicott, and now owned by a descendant of the same name. It is near Danversport Station, and, though very old, seems well preserved. The famous old pear tree, planted in 1630 by Governor Endicott, is still to be seen in a field not far from the house. It now bears fruit and shows as to its upper branches a good degree of vigor, notwithstanding its trunk has been sadly riven and blasted by the storms and winds of more than two and a half centuries.

Danvers.

On Centre Street, near Newbury, may be seen an interesting old house, the birthplace of Colonel Israel Hutchinson, built in 1726. The Colonel was a brave and famous fighter, and much esteemed by Washington. He went to Maine with an expedition against the Indians; was in the action at Ticonderoga; scaled the Heights of Abraham with General Wolfe; led a company of "Minute-men" April 19, 1775, and was prominent in the siege of Boston.

A monument to the memory of Colonel Hutchinson has recently been unveiled at the site of his *home*, Danversport. On Forest Street stands the Ambrose Hutchinson House, built in 1708; on Maple Street, the Jesse Putnam House, built about 1750, where Mrs. Jesse Putnam died at the age of one hundred and two years. The Haines House, which stands on Centre Street, was built about 1650. The Ann Putnam House is still standing on the old Middletown road. Ann Putnam, at the age of twelve years, was probably the chief cause of the witchcraft trouble of the time.

Sixty years after the battle of Lexington the citizens of Danvers erected a granite monument to the memory of her seven sons, who fell in the battle, April 19, 1775. It stands on Main Street at the head of Washington, Peabody.

Topsfield.

THE PARSON CAPEN HOUSE.

Topsfield was settled in 1639 by people from Ipswich and Salem, it being a part of the latter, or Naumkeag, till 1650, when it was incorporated under its present name. Previous to its becoming a separate town it was known as the "New Meadows."

Mary Estes and Sarah Wildes of this town were executed as witches in 1692, during the strange witchcraft delusion.

Here are to be seen a considerable number of pre-Revolutionary houses, the oldest and most interesting one being the Parson Capen House, built in 1686 by the Rev. Joseph

Capen, who removed to Topsfield from Dorchester in 1683. It is noticeable for its second story overhang in front and *third* story overhang at the end. It is still occupied and is in good preservation, though it was never painted. This suggests the query, why should we paint our houses? Think of improving the rich, mellow tints of time by painting this fine old antique!

Every one in town knows the old house, which is reached by a five minutes' walk from the railroad station

THE SALTONSTALL-WHIPPLE HOUSE.

One is inclined at once to grant any claim to old age that might be made for this house, for never have we seen one bearing more striking evidences of early origin. It claims to have been built in 1633, the year of the settlement, thus antedating by one year the "Old Fort" of Medford. It has walls of brick and stone, hidden from view (like those of the Adams houses) by an outer covering of boards. The smallness of the panes of glass and the extreme length of the "lean-to" are very noticeable.

Other Ipswich houses of Colonial times are the Bond House (1640), the Dodge House (1640), the Norton House (1650), the Caldwell House (1660), the Whittlesey House (1640), and probably one or more others.

THE HILL-BOARDMAN HOUSE.

This house fairly caps the climax! It is sufficiently picturesque and antique to please the most fastidious connoisseur of things old. It is not only a "lean-to" of an extreme type, but is also an "overhang," whose principal roof is formed by a sort of double reversal of the "gambrel" style.

For more than two hundred and fifty years it has overlooked the same beautiful landscape in North Saugus.

This house has been made the subject of a fine etching with an imaginary river in front.

A WOLF PIT.

Partly owing to the fact that Lynn was practically an inland town, in consequence of the shallowness of the waters of her harbor, few important events in Colonial history took place here.

The city, or, more properly, the beautiful Walden Park, contains at least two relics of "ye olden tyme" of much interest to students of our early history. These are the wolf pits, of which history states there were many in the Colonies. If there are any others in existence at the present time, the writer has never heard of them.

By means of rude measurements made by the author, these were ascertained to be about eight feet in length, six or seven feet in depth, by two feet in width. They are walled up in a very substantial manner, as may be judged from the fact that they have retained their original form admirably during all the years since 1630.

It is commendable that the city has them protected by means of substantial iron fences.

It is not difficult to find the Wolf Pits when one has reached the foot of Walden Pond. The excellent road on the north side of the pond very soon brings one to a "woods" road diverging toward the north and marked "To the Wolf Pits."

THE BLANEY HOUSE.

Swampscott, formerly a part of Lynn, has its full share of the picturesque and the beautiful. It can also point to some things ancient. For example, at 290 Humphrey Street, we find the Blaney House. This house was built in 1640 by a Captain King. He sold it soon after to John Blaney, whose heirs still own it. Its inner walls are of stone.

The Humphrey House, recently removed, is now 99 Paradise Road. It was built in 1634 by John Humphrey, of wood and bricks brought from Scotland, some of the bricks bearing the name "Cumbernauld," a town near Glasgow.

John Humphrey's wife, Susan, was a daughter of the Earl of Lincoln. He was chosen an Assistant soon after his arrival, and received a grant of five hundred acres of land in Lynn, now Lynnfield, including the beautiful pond that now bears his name.

He returned to England in 1641.

Charlestown.

In passing in review the more important historic spots of Boston and vicinity there can be no more fitting climax than that furnished by the history of the battle of

Bunker Hill.

Since then this spot has witnessed two magnificent and inspiring pageants, the one being the occasion of the laying of the corner-stone of

BUNKER HILL MONUMENT.

General Lafayette was present, and Daniel Webster delivered a dedicatory oration.

Among his memorable sayings at this time is:

"Let it rise till it meet the sun in its coming; let the earliest light of the morning gild it, and parting day linger and play on its summit."

"The celebration," says Frothingham, "was unequaled in magnificence by anything of the kind that had been seen in New England."

Conspicuous honor was paid to forty survivors of the battle who were present.

The second great pageant was the celebration in honor of the completion of the monument, Daniel Webster again being the orator, and the president of the United States, John Tyler, honoring the occasion by his presence.

"Before the orator and around him," says the historian quoted above, "was an immense concourse of people. A hundred thousand, at least, had gathered on the hallowed spot."

The monument stands on the ground inclosed by the redoubt defended by Colonel Prescott on June 17, 1775. It is an obelisk of Quincy granite 30 feet square at the base and 15 feet square near the top, is 220 feet high, and cost about $120,000.

During the battle of Bunker Hill the British set fire to the town, destroying nearly all the houses, most of those that escaped being on Mill Street.

The oldest now standing in the city is a three-story wooden building numbered 201 Main Street, and bears on its front a tablet with the following inscription :

HERE WAS BORN
SAMUEL FINLEY BREESE MORSE,
27 APRIL, 1791,
INVENTOR OF THE
ELECTRIC TELEGRAPH.

Professor Morse was graduated at Yale in 1810, studied art in England under Benjamin West, and designed an electric telegraph in 1832. Congress granted him an appropriation for a line between Baltimore and Washington, which was completed in 1844.

Within a year there has been dug up on the grounds of this old house a solid six-pound cannon shot, — a grim reminder of the battle.

The first settlement in Charlestown was in 1628.

The town became a city in 1847, and was annexed to Boston in 1873.

MISCELLANEOUS OLD HOUSES.

The search for old houses and historic spots has greatly grown upon us year by year, and proved a much more fruitful subject than we had previously supposed possible. One notes with pleasure the existence still of interesting old houses in nearly every town on the coast from Plymouth to Portland.

The only house now standing in Plymouth at any time occupied by a member of the Mayflower Pilgrims is the Howland House, built in 1666. The Doten House, however, is six years older, and stands on Sandwich Street. In Sandwich is still standing and well preserved, the Tupper House. It is pleasant to look upon, but we have not been able to learn its history.

Burlington has the famous Samuel Sewall House, built before 1751. It is on Lexington road, about a fourth of a mile from the meeting-house, and noted as the place of concealment of Hancock and Adams after their flight from Lexington, April 19, 1775.

In Duxbury we find two especially interesting old houses,— the Alden House, built in 1653, and occupied by nine generations of Aldens, and the Standish House, built by a son of Myles Standish in 1666, partly from timbers saved from the burning of the house of his father.

Winthrop has an interesting old house, built in 1649 by Deane Winthrop, son of the good Governor John Winthrop. It is on Shirley Street, near Ocean Spray station.

Marblehead contains half a dozen or more old houses, the most famous being that of Colonel Jeremiah Lee, on Washington Street, near Abbot Hall. It is a massive, three-story brick building, and otherwise remarkable for having a hallway about eighteen feet square.

Great changes are often made by the "march of improvement"; sometimes equally great changes are made by the very reverse of "improvement."

One dislikes to see the homes of famous men elbowed and shouldered and crowded by their more pretentious neighbors. Such is the fate of a house, now numbered 342½ Hanover Street, near the corner of Bennett, built by Increase Mather in 1677, and in it his son Cotton was born. The Mather tomb is in Copp's Hill-burying ground.

The Clough-Vernon House,

is a good specimen of overhang, situated on Vernon Place, off Charter Street, and was built before 1698.

The Blake House

stands in the rear of Cottage Street, Dorchester, and was built in 1650 by Elder James Blake, a man prominent in the affairs of the town, as is shown in a continuous service in some official capacity for more than twenty-five years.

The Aspinwall House

is perhaps the most famous old house of which the town of Brookline can boast. It was built in 1660 by Peter Aspinwall, has always been owned by some member of the family, and stands on Aspinwall Avenue. William Aspinwall, born in Brookline in 1743 (presumably in the old house above mentioned), was a physician of note, fought as a volunteer in the battle of Lexington, and became a surgeon in the Revolutionary Army.

The Peak House

of Medfield has been admired, talked about, written up, and illustrated in magazines and histories repeatedly, and the impression given that it is the sole survivor of the torch of the Indians of King Philip in 1676. The mistake arises probably from the extreme quaintness of its shape. It was probably built about 1762.

Medway was a part of Medfield till 1713, when it was incorporated as a separate town, the Charles River forming the boundary between the two.

Here is to be seen in good condition the

Clark House

built in 1710, and now occupied by Putnam R. Clark.

It will be of interest, at least to young folks, to remember that "Oliver Optic" (William T. Adams) was born here.

Marshfield has the Governor Winslow House, built in 1650, which was for a time the home of Daniel Webster.

Lincoln has the Whitman House, built in 1700. It is two miles from the center of the town, on the road from Waltham to Stowe. Also a half mile from the Center, on the Lexington road, the "L" part of the Flint House is still standing, and is supposed to be two hundred and fifty years old.

Andover has, among several old houses, that of the famous Anne Bradstreet, a relationship with whom has been claimed by Richard H. Dana, Oliver Wendell Holmes, and William Ellery Channing. This house is supposed to have been built in 1667.

Let the American youth never forget that they possess a noble inheritance, bought by the toils and the sufferings and blood of their ancestors. — JOSEPH STORY.

www.ingramcontent.com/pod-product-compliance
Lightning Source LLC
Chambersburg PA
CBHW022124160426
43197CB00009B/1147